TOWARDS AN
INDEPENDENT WALES

TOWARDS AN INDEPENDENT WALES

Report of the
Independence Commission

January 2021

First impression: 2020
Second edition: 2021
© The Independence Commission & Y Lolfa Cyf., 2020

Cover design: Y Lolfa
Cover picture: FfotoNant

ISBN: 978-1-80099-041-8

Published and printed in Wales
on paper from well-maintained forests by
Y Lolfa Cyf., Talybont, Ceredigion SY24 5HE
e-mail ylolfa@ylolfa.com
website www.ylolfa.com
tel 01970 832 304
fax 832 782

Contents

Introduction to the Second Edition

THIS NEW EDITION OF our Report, only a little over three months since it was first published in late September 2020, is one indication of the growing interest in an independent Wales. Another has been the growth in support for the cross-party pro-independence organisation Yes Cymru. In the past few months its membership has surged more than six-fold to above 16,000. In no small part this was a response to the London Government's failures in handling the Covid crisis.

The same has been the case in Scotland where First Minister Nicola Sturgeon's steady handling of the pandemic has been in stark contrast to Boris Johnson's blustering performance in Westminster. With support rising in the polls, another referendum on Scottish independence now seems well-nigh inevitable.

Meanwhile, the UK has agreed to a Trade and Cooperation Agreement with the EU that binds it into a relationship which will probably become closer rather than looser as economic reality begins to bite and the need for trans-European collaboration becomes more urgent.

In these circumstances, as Adam Price pointed out in his speech in December 2020 responding to this Report, Wales needs to get to grips sooner rather than later with the issues we raise in this volume: the case for independence, the potential for a radically changed relationship between the nations of Britain, and the need for Wales to develop over time an ever-closer relationship with Europe.

Introduction

THE INDEPENDENCE COMMISSION BEGAN work immediately following the UK general election in December 2019. It was tasked with producing recommendations on ways a Plaid Cymru Government should prepare for holding a referendum on independence. The areas we were asked to examine are contained in our Terms of Reference in Appendix 2.

As we set out in Chapter 2, during the past year there has been a substantial shift in Welsh opinion in favour of independence, which is now polling at around 30 per cent (excluding Don't Knows). The figure is close to 40 per cent if Wales were able to remain in the European Union. Those statistics obscure even more substantial shifts within different segments of the population. So, for example, there is 58 per cent support among 16 to 34-year-olds if Wales could remain a member of the European Union.

Part of the background is a crisis of the British State in relation to Northern Ireland and Scotland, which the 2016 Brexit referendum and the 2019 general election underlined. There is also a rejuvenation of the wider Welsh independence movement, with YesCymru among a number of new initiatives gathering momentum.

Plaid Cymru is a political party whose main objective is to form a government. Indeed, that will be its principal contribution to our gaining independence. However, Plaid is confronted with the dilemma of winning an election when a majority of the electorate does not yet support its principal aim of independence.

In 2007, the SNP's solution to that dilemma was to park the independence question by saying it would be subject to a referendum, and so was not part of its immediate plans for forming a government. Of course, the SNP went on to win a majority at the subsequent 2011 election, and that was then followed by the Scottish independence referendum in 2014.

So, the purpose of the Independence Commission is to help with the longer-term work of preparing the ground for independence, while Plaid Cymru simultaneously prepares a more immediate Programme for Government in 2021.

The Commission also has the role of addressing the questions and concerns of those we might call Indy Curious – people who have accepted much of the emotional arguments for independence, but still, quite legitimately, have serious questions about the practical case.

When Adam Price addressed the Commission's first meeting, in Cardiff in December 2019, he argued that Wales is in a similar position to where Scotland was a decade or so ago, but is catching up at an accelerating pace:

> "I see a vacuum between where we are politically and
> the development of opinion on independence. The
> Independence Commission has a major role in responding
> to that vacuum, by addressing many of the questions that are
> flowing into it."

The biggest question of all is economics. Whether Wales can afford independence doesn't come up in the same way as it has in the past, for example, in such terms as whether we are simply too poor to be self-governing. Instead, it now tends to be expressed in terms of the 'fiscal gap'. Would we able to continue to pay for public services, such as education and the NHS, and to provide pensions at the level to which we are accustomed?

Of course, this is directly related to our underlying economic performance as a nation. So, the Commission was asked to provide recommendations on actions a Plaid Welsh Government should put in train during the 2020s to reduce the fiscal gap, and so prepare the ground for independence.

But there are many other questions, too, and the Commission has dealt with those we think that should have priority for an incoming Plaid Cymru Government. In particular, we have given a lot of attention to the relationships an independent Wales should seek to forge with our immediate neighbours, those within the British Isles, and also in the European Union.

We are firmly of the view that the long-term destiny of an independent Wales should be as a full member of the European Union. Given the Brexit vote in 2016, and its aftermath, there is no immediate prospect of that. However, we have made recommendations on how Wales should forge closer relations with the European Union, both in the run-up to achieving independence and afterwards.

Whatever constitutional status Wales achieves in the future, we will always share our island with our English and Scottish friends. It makes sense for us to seek the closest possible relationships, but on the basis of equality and not in the subordinate position that has been the case for much of our history. As a Commission we have spent a good deal of time exploring how that might be best achieved in constitutional terms, though not at the expense of retaining our essential sovereignty and also maintaining close European ties.

In our report we re-examine the, by now, urgent necessity for Wales to attain its own distinctive jurisdiction. We also judge there is a need for Wales to create a Welsh Public Service that would embrace officials working for local government, the health service and other public services. This aspect was not in our Terms of Reference, but in the course of our work we discovered this to be necessary if a Plaid Cymru Government is to be successful in the 2020s.

We have set out a framework for developing our own Welsh Constitution and suggested an outline for its shape and content. This we recommend should be developed more fully through a widespread consultation process ahead of an independence referendum. We believe a constitution arrived at in this way will give the people of Wales reassurance about the values that will guide an independent Wales.

We recommend that a Plaid Cymru Government should pass enabling legislation, a Self-Determination (Wales) Bill, in its first term. This would establish by statute a Standing National Commission whose role would be to provide an objective source of information on all aspects of independence, so that when the referendum takes place the people of Wales will be able to make an informed choice. For example, the Commission should undertake a series of Citizens' Assemblies across Wales to generate an informed debate. The Commission should also advise on the holding of the referendum, and the question or questions to be asked.

In the report's final chapter we set out a framework of values we believe an independent Wales should adopt. They are calculated to unite the people of Wales and build confidence in our future prospects as a fair-minded, environmentally-aware and prosperous nation, committed to social justice and peace and security in the world.

The Commission has undertaken most of its work in the midst of the Covid-19 pandemic. This has prevented us from embarking on as much consultation about our thinking as we had planned. However, we have managed to have a number of meetings with people with expertise on a variety of constitutional, political, economic and financial aspects relating to independence that have proved invaluable. Among those with whom we have consulted are Guto Ifan, Professor Gerry Holtham, Professor Jim Gallagher, Sir Adrian Webb, David Melding MS, Robin McAlpine, Hywel Ceri Jones, Charles Marquand, Mike Russell MSP, Professor Kevin Morgan, and Dafydd Trystan. We have also met with representatives of YesCymru and on three occasions with the House of Lords Constitutional Reform Group, led by the Marquis of Salisbury.

The Covid crisis is widely regarded as having demonstrated the advantages that can accrue from Wales having at least some control over its own affairs. Many of our people have become aware for the first time of the positive advantages for Wales of possessing its own democratic institutions, the Senedd and Welsh Government. The Commission believes that independence, providing much greater control of our own affairs, is the status for which Wales should aim.

Executive summary

1. Wales, with its own Senedd and powers, is already on a journey towards independence. Completing the process will involve agreeing a sovereign constitution. This should be achieved through a series of clear, legal steps, delivered by public servants, including the judiciary, not only within Wales but in other jurisdictions. Sustainability and the well-being of future generations are core Welsh values that should be central to the constitution of an independent Wales.

2. Wales must have a separate Welsh jurisdiction. Independence is not a prerequisite for this, but the general reservation to Westminster of powers relating to the single England and Wales jurisdiction needs to be removed. The recommendations of the Commission on Justice for Wales should be implemented by a Plaid Cymru Government.

3. The people of Wales are central to the independence process and they need to have a clear understanding of the options available for their political future. Ahead of a referendum on independence a statutory National Commission and associated Citizens' Assemblies should be established to ensure maximum awareness, participation, and involvement.

4. The National Commission should test the views of the people of Wales in an initial exploratory referendum, setting out constitutional options. The outcome should be used to

persuade the UK Westminster Government to agree to a binary referendum on the status quo versus the preferred choice expressed in the exploratory referendum.

5. The National Commission will draft a Welsh Constitution in consultation with the widest possible representation of the people of Wales, being mindful of diversity and inclusion, through the Citizens' Assemblies.

6. We are firmly of the view that the long-term destiny of an independent Wales should be as a full member of the European Union. Given the Brexit vote in 2016, and its aftermath, there is no immediate prospect of that. However, we have made recommendations on how Wales should forge closer relations with the European Union, both in the run-up to achieving independence and afterwards.

7. An independent Wales will face practical challenges to becoming a member of the EU if England remains outside, but these can be overcome. The National Commission should examine the potential for an independent Wales, separately from England, joining the European Free Trade Area (Efta), which confers membership of the EU Single Market. As a member of Efta, an independent Wales would be in a position, in its own right, to negotiate a free-trade agreement with England.

8. Regardless of membership, a Plaid Cymru Government should establish a special relationship with the EU. A first priority will be to seek ways of continuing to participate in the EU Erasmus and Horizon programmes, setting out clearly to the people of Wales why this is essential.

9. Wales and Scotland have been in a relationship with England for centuries. We explore a range of options for a radically changed relationship between the three nations, rather than complete separation. Our proposed Statutory National Commission should conduct discussions with

the Scottish Government to address the challenges to achieving a consensus on future relations and structures, including the possibility of a confederal relationship, such as explored in the Benelux and League of the Isles models in this report.

10. The Welsh economy has had chronic structural weaknesses imposed upon it for a long time and they are challenging. In this report we explain that Wales has failed to make economic progress not because the country is too small or too poor, but because it is trapped within an economy overwhelmingly shaped in the interests of the City of London. This flawed model has failed to deliver prosperity to Wales and offers no expectation of doing so in the future. An independent Wales would be free to change this. It would no longer be a region subordinated to the interests of London and the south east of England or be subject to the fiscal policies determined by the UK Government.

11. There are lessons to be learned from Ireland, formerly one of the most peripheral and poorest parts of the UK. It is now a confident, self-assured independent nation, one of the richest parts of these Isles, with a seat at the United Nations

12. New agencies should be established to promote small business growth, medium-size business development, inward investment, productivity, and export activity. The focus of inward investment should be on businesses capable of offering high quality jobs, in technology, health and sophisticated consumer-facing products. Contact should be deepened with alumni of Welsh universities based overseas. In the aftermath of the Covid-19 crisis greater emphasis on local production and procurement should also be given.

13. An incoming Government should review the entire Welsh

higher education sector to ensure that meeting the needs of the Welsh economy and society is its priority. It should set in motion measures to encourage more Welsh students to stay in Wales for their qualifications and their subsequent careers, and that those going elsewhere are encouraged to return.

14. There should be more collective and cohesive decision-making within the Welsh Cabinet over the setting of the budget and cross-departmental working. A strategic delivery plan for a Programme of Government, with an agreed annual timetable and targets across the five-year term, should be put in place. The Finance Department should take on a greater Treasury role and, working closely with the First Minister's Office, deliver greater co-ordination of policy delivery according to targets across the whole of the Welsh Government.

15. The role of the Welsh civil service should be re-examined, leading to a separation of economic policymaking and implementation. Welsh Government should develop proposals and a timetable for the creation of a Public Service for Wales, with a shared culture, grades and pay scales across all public sector organisations, including the Welsh Government's civil service. To this end, the reservation to Westminster of powers relating to the civil service needs to be removed.

Main recommendations

A Welsh jurisdiction

1. Wales is developing its own body of laws and should have a separate jurisdiction.

2. The Welsh Government should begin the process of reform, leading to a separate Welsh jurisdiction. This can be put into effect while the current scheme of devolution continues by implementing the Commission on Justice for Wales's recommendations. However, the reservation to Westminster of the single jurisdiction needs to be removed.

3. Arrangements should be made for the Senedd to monitor and review the process of reform.

4. A single portfolio, a Minister for Justice separate from that of the Counsel General, should be created, bringing together the diverse and unco-ordinated justice functions currently held by the Welsh Government.

5. The Minister of Justice should set out a pathway for implementation and take a leadership role across all sectors in driving forward the Commission on Justice in Wales' recommendations for creating a separate Welsh legal jurisdiction.

Effective government and the civil service

1. The appointment of the Welsh Permanent Secretary should be made by the First Minister of Wales on the advice of an independent Welsh Civil Service Commission.

2. Within the Cabinet there should be a more collective and cohesive decision-making process over the setting of the budget and cross-departmental working. This should entail putting in place a strategic delivery plan for the Programme of Government, with an agreed annual timetable and targets across the five-year term.

3. The Finance Department should take on a greater Treasury role and, working closely with the First Minister's Office, deliver greater co-ordination of policy delivery according to targets across the whole of the Welsh Government.

4. A central Policy Unit should be set up within the First Minister's Office to work on strategic questions and ensure delivery across departments.

5. The role of the senior civil service should be re-defined as that of leading change that will benefit Wales – rather than managing the machine and protecting the status quo.

6. Welsh Government should develop proposals and a timetable for the creation of a Public Service for Wales, with a shared culture, grades and pay scales across all public sector organisations, including the Welsh Government's civil service. This would require that the reservation to Westminster of powers relating to the civil service be removed.

7. The Welsh Government's Academi Wales should become a National School of Public Management and Governance, attached to the Welsh university sector. It should have an increased budget, a Board of Directors to include the Permanent Secretary and an independent Chair. It should develop an international research programme related to small country governance and enter into partnership arrangements with other management schools such as the Kennedy School of Government at Harvard and Insead.

Addressing the fiscal gap

1.   The role of the Welsh civil service should be re-examined to separate economic policymaking and implementation.

2.   A new agency or agencies should be established to promote small business growth, medium size business development, inward investment, productivity, and export activity.

3.   A new inward investment focus is needed on businesses capable of offering high quality jobs, even if initially in small numbers, in technology, health and sophisticated consumer-facing products. Potential investors in new technology nations need to be cultivated and contact deepened with alumni of Welsh universities overseas.

4.   The export propensity of Welsh firms needs to be encouraged and stimulated to increase revenues and help increase the productivity and scale of Welsh business. Wales should search for businesses that might be relocated back in Britain for strategic security, environmental or other reasons.

5.   The role of the Welsh Development Bank should be expanded to ensure that state support for key sectors can take the form of direct Welsh Government stakes.

6.   Greater involvement with the venture capital industry should be sought and a Welsh venture capital trust investing in Welsh start-ups established.

7.   The foundation economy should be put at the centre of policymaking and incentives and penalties to secure greater public sector purchasing put in place. A wholesaler type body should be created to aggregate private sector provision and support tendering, together with a facility through which companies could make their offering more widely known.

8.   In the aftermath of the Covid-19 crisis, a window for a much

greater emphasis on local production and procurement will open and this must be seized. Support should be given to businesses seeking to re-shore products currently made elsewhere, and further efforts made to ensure Welsh food producers contribute a bigger share of the nation's food purchases.

9. An incoming Government should review the entire Welsh higher education sector to ensure its priority is meeting the needs of the Welsh economy and society. It should set in motion measures to encourage more Welsh students to stay in Wales for their degrees and their subsequent careers, and that those going elsewhere are encouraged to return.

10. Policymakers need to be equipped with better business intelligence on the needs of the Welsh economy. Welsh Government and business should back the creation of a new university centre for the study of Welsh business and business needs.

Wales and Europe

1. The Welsh Government should use the Trade and Cooperation Agreement reached between the UK and the EU at the end of 2020, to develop close bilateral relationships between Wales and the EU.

2. A Plaid Cymru Government should build upon Wales's existing International Strategy by:

   - Strengthening Wales's presence in Brussels through Wales House.

   - Developing existing partnerships with European nations and regions and examine the scope for adding to their number.

3. The Welsh Government should establish a central unit as part of the Cabinet Office to deal with international

affairs and, in particular, to drive a strong and consistent policy for European engagement.

4. A Plaid Cymru Government should establish a special relationship with the EU as representing a nation aspiring to become independent and an accessor state. A priority should be to seek ways of continuing to participate in the EU Erasmus and Horizon programmes. Secondly, a Plaid Cymru Government should develop a process that puts Wales on a path towards meeting the 35 Chapters of Accession to the European Union.[1]

5. A Plaid Cymru Government should examine the scope for reaching agreement with the European Commission to enable specified products from Wales to have unfettered access to the Single Market. An inspectorate could be established to certify that products of Welsh companies participating in the scheme complied fully with EU regulations. A further possibility would be to establish a port which would export only goods in this category and where entry to the EU would be allowed without formalities.

6. In developing its relations with the European Union, a Plaid Cymru Government should pay particular attention to cultivating a close partnership with Ireland.

Relations with our neighbours: options for an independent Wales

1. Plaid Cymru should retain its commitment to an independent Wales becoming a member of the European Union.

2. Federalism, being promoted by elements within the UK unionist parties as an alternative to Welsh and Scottish independence, is impractical since England comprises 87 per cent of the UK population, while there is no plan

or desire to divide England into regional territories, particularly with legislative powers.

3. The statutory National Commission should conduct discussions with the Scottish Government with a view to arriving at a consensus on future relations and structures between the nations of Britain.

4. The statutory National Commission should establish contacts with Benelux in order to consider the applicability of its confederal model to a reconstituted Britain, recognising that Belgium, Netherlands and Luxembourg are members of the EU.

5. The statutory National Commission should conduct an examination into which policy fields might be delegated to the centre within a confederation such as outlined in the Benelux and League of the Isles models.

6. By pooling aspects of their sovereignty in a confederal relationship, the countries of Britain have an opportunity to achieve a more evenly distributed and hence improved economic performance. If they do so at the same time as furthering relations with the European Union, they also have an opportunity to enhance their presence and prestige on the world stage.

7. The statutory National Commission should examine the possibility of Wales, separately from England, joining Efta and the EEA.

A constitution for an independent Wales

1. The path to an independent Wales with its own constitution should be a constitutional one. It should be achieved by a series of steps, the legality of which should be clear, and the provisions of which would therefore be recognised and enforced by public servants, including the judiciary, not only within Wales but in other jurisdictions.

2. Basic principles of the Welsh Constitution (to be defined in a Bill of Rights) should include:
    - Democracy.
    - Subsidiarity – that is, the principle that actions by the state can only be justified in order to achieve desirable social outcomes that cannot be achieved as effectively by individual efforts, and that such actions should always be taken at the most local level compatible with the effective achievement of the outcomes in question.
    - The Rule of Law.
    - Equality of all people.
    - Individual and collective freedom.
    - Sustainability – that is, the principle that the needs of the present are to be met without harming the well-being of future generations by compromising the ability of those generations to meet their own needs.

3. Other characteristics of a Welsh Constitution should include:
    - A declaration that Welsh sovereignty rests with the people of Wales.
    - That it should include a description and role of Welsh governing institutions as well as the rights and responsibilities of citizens.
    - That those rights and responsibilities should extend beyond the purely political and legalistic to encompass social and economic rights and responsibilities.
    - That it should draw on best practice from around the world, especially constitutions that have been drawn up for small nations in analogous positions to that of Wales.

4. The Elements of a Welsh Constitution, as recommended

by the Commission, represent an outline of the kind of Wales that could be achieved once Wales is independent.

5. The precise details of a Welsh Constitution will need to be discussed and agreed by the people of Wales and their representatives. This will be necessary to achieve the level of consensus and certainty which are essential if a constitution is to fulfil its purpose as the basic law of the state.

A Welsh Self-Determination Bill

1. A key commitment in Plaid Cymru's Manifesto for the 2021 Senedd election should be setting up a statutory National Commission – to include holding Citizens' Assemblies – to inform the people of Wales about options for their constitutional future.

2. A Bill to establish the Commission with a broad remit, leaving it to subordinate legislation to settle the detail, is recommended as the best way forward. This would limit the disruptive effects of potential challenges on the grounds of competence, while preserving a measure of independence for the Commission and a meaningful role for the Senedd. An outline structure for such a draft Bill is set out in Appendix 1.

3. The Bill should be drafted to include a purpose clause, making it clear that neither the Bill nor any of its provisions relate to the union of the nations of Wales and England.

4. It should be the Commission rather than Ministers in the Government that is authorised in the legislation to undertake a plebiscite on the future governance options for Wales.

5. The Commission should explore the New Zealand approach to testing the views of the people of Wales in an initial exploratory referendum, setting out constitutional

options. It should be made clear that the outcome will be used to persuade the UK Westminster Government to agree to a binary referendum on the status quo versus the preferred choice in the first referendum.

CHAPTER 1

Building the road

THE BASQUES HAVE A saying about their history of constitutional development: "We build the road as we travel". This is certainly the case with the Welsh experience, which has taken more than a century of struggle to reach a position where independence is now a serious prospect.

The story begins in the late 19th century, with the great extension of the franchise which bore fruit at the election of 1868. Certainly, that election brought to the fore a large number of Liberal MPs representative of Welsh aspirations. On this count we should identify the true beginning of the process as 1886, the year when Cymru Fydd (Young Wales) was established to campaign for 'Home Rule' for Wales. Led by the Liberal politicians Lloyd George and T. E. Ellis, it was a creature of its time, seeing greater autonomy as giving Wales equality with the other 'Home Nations' within the British Empire. Like so much else the First World War undermined this outlook. Saunders Lewis, the founder of Plaid Cymru in 1925, propagated an entirely different vision of Wales as a free nation within a European framework.

The 20th century

For much of the 20th century, the achievement of Welsh constitutional aspirations was largely confined to administrative devolution, beginning with the creation of the Welsh Board for

Education in 1907, followed by a Welsh Insurance Commission in 1911, and a Welsh Board of Health and a Welsh Department in the Ministry of Agriculture in 1919.

The early 20th century also witnessed the creation of many important new national institutions, notably the University of Wales, the National Library and National Museum. By 1945 there were 15 government departments with offices in Wales, but no territorial department, as there was in Scotland. During the 1930s and 1940s there were a number of campaigns in favour of a Welsh Office headed by a Secretary of State for Wales in the British Cabinet. The 1945-50 Labour Government rejected this proposal. Instead, in 1948 it established an unelected, advisory Council for Wales and Monmouthshire.

In 1951, a new junior government post of Minister of State for Welsh Affairs was created by the Conservative Government, initially as a junior minister in the Home Office and from 1957 as a post held jointly with the Ministry of Housing and Local Government.

In the early 1950s the first campaign for a Parliament for Wales collected a petition of 250,000 signatures. In 1955, a Private Member's Bill advocating a Parliament was proposed by S. O. Davies, Labour MP for Merthyr, but defeated by 64 votes to 16. The following year the Council for Wales and Monmouthshire presented a detailed case for bringing together the various government offices in Wales into a new Welsh Office, comparable with the Scottish Office. When the Prime Minister Harold Macmillan refused to accede to these arguments the Council resigned *en bloc*. Its chairman, trade union leader Huw T. Edwards, resigned from the Labour Party and joined Plaid Cymru.

In 1964 the incoming Labour Government established the Welsh Office. At first, its responsibilities were confined to housing, local government and roads. But by 1973 other areas

– including education and training, health, environment and agriculture, economic planning and trade and industry – were added. The Welsh Office had to wait until the late 1970s before its chief civil servant was given the same Permanent Secretary status as those leading other Whitehall departments.

In 1966 a Royal Commission chaired by Lord Beeching was established to examine the court system in England and Wales. Its initial, draft report proposed the division of England and Wales into regions, with Wales being divided between the northern and western regions of England. However, following a campaign led by Welsh lawyers, the final report in 1969 acknowledged that "the special circumstances in Wales" should require the circuit to be treated as a single unit and to be administered from Cardiff.

The election of Plaid Cymru's Gwynfor Evans in the Carmarthen by-election in 1966, followed by the Hamilton by-election victory of the SNP's Winnie Ewing in 1967, led to the setting up of the Royal Commission on the Constitution. When it reported in 1973 the Commission recommended the creation of elected Assemblies for Wales and Scotland. This proposal was decisively rejected by a four-to-one majority in the Welsh referendum held on 1 March 1979. Nonetheless, the holding of the referendum conceded the principle that sovereignty over their constitutional future lay with the people of Wales.

The 1980s were to prove a highly significant decade in the political history of Wales, due to events that fundamentally changed the outlook of the people. The 1984-5 Miners' Strike was seminal. Although the miners were defeated, the experience demonstrated both solidarity of support across Wales, and also led to a widespread conviction that in the last resort Wales should learn to take responsibility for its own future. In addition, the role of the Conservative Government, led by Margaret Thatcher, coupled with its low level of support in Wales in successive elections, demonstrated a democratic deficit and there were renewed calls for Wales to have its own nationally representative institution.

During the 1990s these calls produced stronger cross-party support for an elected Assembly than had been achieved in the 1970s. In 1993, the Campaign for a Welsh Assembly, launched in 1987, rebranded itself as the Parliament for Wales Campaign. By then it had a membership of more than 1,000, including many councils and trade union branches. In March 1994 its Democracy Conference at Llandrindod was attended by 250 delegates.

When Labour returned to power in May 1997 its manifesto contained a commitment to holding a fresh referendum on creating a Welsh Assembly. The White Paper *A Voice for Wales*, published in July 1997, outlined its proposals and on 18 September 1997, a referendum was held. The result was an exceedingly narrow majority of 50.3 per cent in favour, a margin of just 6,721 votes. Nonetheless, a Rubicon had been crossed. Public opinion swiftly moved to support an Assembly with greater powers.

Ron Davies who, as Secretary of State for Wales had overseen the referendum, famously described devolution as "a process not an event".[2] It was a prescient judgement that the first two decades of the 21st century were to demonstrate.

The 21st century

Since the National Assembly was elected in 1999 it has developed its powers incrementally in four phases[3]:

- **Phase One** Executive devolution, under the Government of Wales Act 1998: 1999 to 2007.
- **Phase Two** Separation of powers and restricted powers over primary legislation, under the Government of Wales Act 2006: 2007 to 2011.
- **Phase Three** Full law-making powers following the 2011 Referendum: 2011 to 2017.

- **Phase Four** Senedd moves to reserved powers model following the Wales Act 2017 and acquires tax-raising powers under the Wales Act 2014: 2017 to 2020.

Phase One: Executive devolution 1999–2007

Following the referendum, the UK Parliament passed the Government of Wales Act 1998 that established the National Assembly as a corporate body – with the executive (the government) and the legislature (the Assembly) operating as one. In contrast to the primary law-making powers given to the Scottish Parliament, the Act limited the National Assembly to the making of secondary legislation in specified areas, including agriculture, fisheries, education, housing and highways. These powers were broadly equivalent to those previously held by the Secretary of State for Wales.

The Assembly's single corporate body structure, akin to that of local government, was soon found to be unworkable. In 2002 the Assembly agreed a resolution which separated its executive and legislative functions by creating what was termed the Welsh Assembly Government – to describe the policies and actions of the Cabinet – as distinct from the work of the National Assembly.

In 2002 the cross-party Commission under former Labour politician and European Commissioner Lord (Ivor) Richard, was established and reported in 2004. It recommended the separation of the executive and legislature as individual legal entities, full legislative powers, an increase in the numbers of members from 60 to 80 and their election by the STV system of proportional representation.

In 2005 the Westminster Government published the White Paper *Better Governance for Wales*, its response to the Richard Commission. This rejected the recommendations for more members and proportional representation. However, it proposed to:

- Give legislative effect to a formal separation between the National Assembly and the Welsh Assembly Government.
- Grant the Assembly, in the longer-term, primary law-making powers, although as that would constitute "a fundamental change to the Welsh (devolution) settlement", this would require the support of the Welsh electorate through a referendum.
- Confer on the Assembly, "gradually over a number of years", enhanced legislative powers in defined policy areas, via Orders in Council – subject to Westminster consent – enabling it to modify legislation within its existing executive functions.

Phase Two: Separation of Powers 2007 to 2011

Better Governance for Wales was implemented by the Government of Wales Act 2006 which had three key elements:

- Formal separation between the legislature (National Assembly) and executive (Welsh Assembly Government).
- Permission for the Assembly to pass 'Assembly Measures' (primary legislation) over matters conferred within 20 fields of responsibility on a case-by-case basis through 'Legislative Competence Orders' (LCOs). These required the consent of both Houses of Parliament and the Secretary of State for Wales.
- Granting to the Assembly primary full law-making powers over subjects listed under the 20 defined headings, subject to a referendum.

The new system of Legislative Competence Orders (LCOs) was widely criticised. Barry Morgan, Archbishop of Wales and

Chair of Cymru Yfory/Tomorrow's Wales, a body set up in 2004 to campaign for more powers for the Assembly, described it as "confusing, arcane and cumbersome". In the first two years, only four uncontroversial LCOs were passed, with more contentious measures delayed or, in the case of an attempt to prohibit the 'right to buy' council houses, abandoned.

In 2009 the All-Wales Convention was established under the chairmanship of Sir Emyr Jones Parry, a former UK ambassador to the United Nations, as part of the One Wales Coalition Agreement between Labour and Plaid Cymru. It recommended that a referendum on full law-making powers should be held.

Meanwhile, the 'One Wales' Coalition Agreement also entailed establishing a commission to review the National Assembly's funding and finance, under the chairmanship of economist Gerald Holtham. It recommended a needs-based formula to determine the Assembly's block grant in place of the Barnett population-based formula established in 1979. The commission also called for devolution of tax-varying powers akin to those set out in the Government of Scotland Act 1998. The Barnett formula, Holtham said, lacked "objective justification" and had survived for 30 years "solely for reasons of political and administrative convenience."[4]

Phase Three: Conferred law-making powers 2011 to 2017

Following a referendum on 3 March 2011, the Assembly was given full law-making powers in the twenty policy areas devolved to Wales. A total of 517,132 people (63.5 per cent) voted Yes, and 297,380 (36.5 per cent) voted No, on a turnout of 35.6 per cent.

In October 2011, the Conservative-Liberal coalition government at Westminster established the Commission on

Devolution, chaired by former House of Commons and Assembly Clerk Paul Silk, to examine, in two stages, the Assembly's financial accountability and legislative powers.

Part I of the Silk Commission's brief, on financial powers, was published in November 2012. Its recommendations included:

- Devolution of landfill tax, stamp duty, land tax, the aggregates levy and business rates.
- Transfer of Air Passenger Duty for long-haul flights initially, with full devolution possible in future.
- Responsibility for income tax to be shared between the Assembly and Westminster, with the Welsh Government able to vary income tax within UK rates (with consequent reductions to the block grant).
- Transfer of income tax powers to be conditional upon resolving issues of fair funding (i.e. the Barnett formula), and subject to a referendum.
- Borrowing powers to support increased investment in infrastructure and to manage greater variability in tax revenues.

The UK Government's Wales Act 2014, which transferred further powers to the Assembly, covered the following areas:

- Devolution of stamp duty, business rates and landfill tax to the Assembly, as well as the power to propose completely new taxes subject to approval from both Houses of Parliament and the Secretary of State for Wales.
- A referendum on the devolution of income tax. If affirmative, then the Assembly would be able to set a Welsh rate of income tax, 10p within each UK band (but without the lockstep set out in the Scotland Act 2012).
- Extending Assembly terms from four to five years to avoid clashes with UK general elections following the Fixed-term Parliaments Act 2011.
- Removing the prohibition on candidates in Assembly

elections from contesting both constituency seats and places on the regional list, but prohibiting a "dual mandate", whereby AMs also served as MPs.

- Formally changing the Welsh Assembly Government's name to the Welsh Government (a term in informal use since 2011).
- Allowing Welsh Ministers to limit the amount of debt individual local housing authorities in Wales might hold.
- Requiring the Law Commission to provide advice and information to Welsh Ministers on law reform matters.

In March 2014 Part II of the Silk Commission's report, on legislative powers, was published with recommendations that included:

- An increase in the number of Assembly Members to deal with an 'overstretched' legislature, suggesting 'at least' 80 members.
- Increasing the National Assembly's power to decide on energy projects in Wales, raising the limit to 350 megawatts.
- Regionalisation of governance of the BBC Trust in Wales and responsibility for financing the Welsh language television channel, S4C.
- Devolution of responsibility for the water industry in Wales.
- Devolution of regulatory powers over transport, including ports, railways, buses and taxis, and a greater say in determining the rail franchise in Wales.
- Devolution of responsibility for drink-driving and speed limits.
- Devolution of policing to Wales, as in Scotland and Northern Ireland.
- Devolution of youth justice and a review – in ten years' time – of whether all criminal justice responsibilities should come under Assembly control.

- A move to a Scottish-style 'reserved powers' model of devolution, under which policy areas reserved to the UK were clearly specified, with everything else considered devolved.

In February 2015, a framework 'St David's Day Agreement' was made between the four main political parties and the Secretary of State for Wales which incorporated most of the Part II Silk Commission's recommendations, but not on policing and criminal justice. The Agreement, published as *Powers for a Purpose: Towards a lasting devolution settlement for Wales*, included:

- Energy projects up to 350MW to be decided by Welsh Ministers.
- Power to lower the voting age to 16 for Assembly elections.
- Devolution of all powers relating to Assembly and local government elections.
- A review of Air Passenger Duty with a view to devolving control.

As part of the St David's Day Agreement, the UK Government also agreed that:

- The National Assembly and Welsh Government should formally be recognised in statute as permanent.
- On future votes of constitutional importance – i.e. the size of the Assembly or its electoral system – a 'super-majority' of two-thirds in the Assembly would be required.
- The UK Government would examine which recommendations of the Smith Commission (on Scottish devolution) were relevant to Wales.

In 2016 the Assembly passed the Tax Collection and Management (Wales) Act 2016, in preparation for exercising the taxation and borrowing powers devolved by the Wales Act 2014.

Phase Four: 'Reserved powers' 2017 to 2020

The Wales Act 2017 introduced a 'reserved powers model' similar in concept to the Scottish system, under which the National Assembly can make laws on any matter except those reserved to the UK Parliament. Its key provisions included:

- Moving from a 'conferred' to a 'reserved' model of devolution in Wales and recognising the 'permanence' of the National Assembly.
- Giving Welsh Ministers new executive powers, for example over onshore petroleum licensing, speed limits, pedestrian crossings and traffic signs.
- Creating a President of Welsh tribunals, although England and Wales would continue to share a single jurisdiction.
- Removal of the requirement for a referendum on the devolution of income tax and ending the entitlement of the Secretary of State for Wales "to participate in proceedings of the Assembly but not to vote".

In September 2017, the then First Minister Carwyn Jones established a Commission on Justice in Wales, chaired by Lord Thomas of Cwmgiedd, to review the operation of the justice system in Wales, including the prospect of a separate jurisdiction (which had not formed part of the Wales Act 2017). The Commission reported in October 2019 and recommended the devolution of policing and justice to the National Assembly and the creation of a separate Welsh jurisdiction.

The matters which remain reserved to the UK Parliament are set out in Schedule 7A to the Government of Wales Act 2006. The reservations are split into two categories: general reservations and specific reservations. The general reservations are listed under the following heads:

- The Constitution.
- Public service.
- Political parties.

- Single legal jurisdiction of England and Wales.
- Tribunals.
- Foreign affairs.
- Defence.

The specific reservations are listed under the following heads:

- Financial and Economic matters.
- Home affairs.
- Trade and Industry.
- Energy.
- Transport.
- Social Security, Child Support, Pensions and Compensation.
- Professions.
- Employment.
- Health, Safety and Medicines.
- Media, Culture and Sport.
- Justice.
- Land and Agricultural Assets.
- Miscellaneous.

At the end of the first two decades of the existence of the National Assembly, and despite all the changes that had been made, it was still widely agreed that the devolution settlement remained unnecessarily complex, difficult to understand, less than transparent and lacking in accountability. As the Commission on Justice in Wales reported:

"The complexity of the overall operation of the UK constitution is reflected in the fact that despite Wales moving to a similar reserved powers system of devolution to that in Scotland and Northern Ireland, there are major differences in the list of matters reserved to Westminster as compared to the two other legislatures. The Government of Wales Act 2006 as amended contains 44 pages of reservations and restrictions, compared with 17 pages in the Scotland Act 1998."[5]

And as the Assembly's Constitutional and Legislative Affairs Committee concluded in its report on the Wales Bill that preceded the Wales Act 2017, it was not "a lasting or durable settlement":

"We do not believe that the Bill's proposed model of legislative competence is clear, coherent and workable, or will provide a durable framework within which the National Assembly can legislate. As a consequence, we consider legislators in the UK Parliament and in the National Assembly will need to return to address these matters sooner rather than later."[6]

In November 2017, the Expert Panel on Assembly Electoral Reform, chaired by Professor Laura McAllister, recommended that the Assembly "should be increased to at least 80 Members, and preferably closer to 90 Members, to ensure that the parliament elected in 2021 has sufficient capacity to fulfil its policy, legislative and financial scrutiny responsibilities"[7].

In September 2019 the Labour Welsh Government published a paper outlining its constitutional aspirations. It opened with the following declaration:

"Whatever its historical origins, the United Kingdom is best seen now as a voluntary association of nations taking the form of a multi-national state, whose members share and redistribute resources and risks among themselves to advance their common interests. Wales is committed to this association, which must be based on the recognition of popular sovereignty in each part of the UK; Parliamentary sovereignty as traditionally understood no longer provides a sound foundation for this evolving constitution."[8]

In February 2020 the Senedd and Elections (Wales) Act 2020 became law. It lowered the voting age for Assembly elections to 16 and changed the name of the Assembly to Senedd Cymru or Welsh Parliament, commonly known as the Senedd.

CHAPTER 2

Public attitudes

During April 2020, Plaid Cymru commissioned the polling company Survation to undertake an on-line survey with 3,039 respondents on a wide range of electoral and policy themes. Among the matters explored were questions relating to the Welsh language and identity and views on Welsh independence. A summary of the responses is reported here, and in the case of independence, evidence from other YouGov polls conducted in the past year.

Welsh identity

More than two thirds (69 percent) of respondents to the Survation poll said they have no proficiency in the Welsh language. Around one in four (24 per cent) could understand spoken Welsh, while 17 percent could speak it. A further 20 per cent could read Welsh, and 14 per cent write it.

However, there was an encouraging increase in proficiency among younger generations. Roughly half (48 per cent) of 16 to 34-year-olds said they could either read, write, speak or understand Welsh, contrasting to the 80 per cent of over-55s who said they could do none of these.

Respondents in north Wales were more likely to have some level of Welsh than those from any other region, with 44 per cent saying they were able to perform at least one of the functions listed.

In the other regions, between 65 and 78 per cent of respondents said they had no proficiency in Welsh.

Of those who could speak Welsh, 44 per cent described themselves as fluent and 40 per cent said they speak the language every day (70 per cent say they spoke it at least once a week).

A majority (56 per cent) of those currently intending to vote Plaid with their constituency vote in the 2021 Senedd elections had some level of Welsh, while the opposite was true for supporters of all other parties.

When respondents were asked to describe their national identity, allowing for multiple choices, 55 per cent said Welsh, 33 per cent said British and 22 per cent selected English. Mirroring the findings of the questions on Welsh language ability, the young were much more likely than older generations to describe their identity as Welsh, with 62 per cent saying so, a figure which fell to 56 per cent among 35 to 54-year-olds and 48 per cent for those over 55.

There was a corresponding rise in a sense of British identity as we move up the generations: whereas just over a quarter of 16 to 34-year-olds would call themselves British, 34 per cent and 38 per cent of those aged 35-54 and 55+ would do so. Majorities of prospective Plaid (76 per cent) and Labour (65 per cent) voters identified as Welsh.

In an effort to ascertain how deeply felt particular identities were held, respondents were asked whether they identified as exclusively Welsh or British, more one than the other, or equally Welsh and British. In total, only one in five (20 per cent) said they felt no attachment at all to a Welsh identity. This rose to 25 per cent among the oldest cohort and fell to 13 per cent among the young. Overall, there was a relatively even split between those who felt exclusively Welsh or more Welsh than British (39 per cent), and those who felt more or exclusively British (33 per cent).

Independence

For some years a variety of polling questions have been asked of the Welsh electorate about independence, with responses ranging from under 5 per cent support to more than 40 per cent. This wide range of support has to some extent reflected different polling methodologies, and particularly the specific wording of the question asked.

However, the polling during the past year has provided more clarity. YouGov has undertaken three recent surveys which included questions on independence – in November 2019, January 2020, and June 2020. In addition, the Plaid Cymru-commissioned Survation poll, in April 2020, asked comparable questions on independence.

The YouGov polls posed an independence referendum question, a constitutional preference question, and a 0-10 or 0-100 scale question on feelings towards independence. The Survation poll also asked the independence referendum question as well as two more hypothetical questions: about how people might vote if Wales could rejoin the EU, and another option where some level of British Isles co-operation might continue.

Independence: the referendum question

Participants in both the YouGov and Survation polls were asked:

"If there was a referendum tomorrow on Wales becoming an independent country and this was the question, how would you vote? Should Wales be an independent country?"

	Nov 2019 YouGov	Jan 2020 YouGov	April 2020 Survation	June 2020 YouGov	August 2020 Survation
Yes	28%	27%	31%	32%	32%
No	72%	73%	69%	68%	68%

(Note: these figures are adjusted by removing those who answered 'Don't know')

On the standard referendum question we find modest growth in support for independence in the past year. However, when compared with the previous decade or so this is a significant uplift, with support more than doubling. Certainly in the period since the last Senedd election in 2016, support for independence has achieved something of a breakthrough, to a point that it must now be regarded as mainstream and more than a marginal prospect. This is underlined when the vote is broken down by party allegiance. So, in the April 2020 Survation poll, 44 per cent of Labour supporters supported independence, as shown in the following table.

	LAB	CON	PC	BREX	LD	Others
Yes	44%	7%	68%	19%	36%	9%
No	56%	93%	32%	81%	64%	91%

Part of the explanation for the rise in support may be the political turbulence caused by the acrimonious Brexit debates since the 2016 referendum that have resulted in a polarising of views on constitutional matters. This is supported by the hypothetical question posed in the April Survation poll on membership of the European Union, namely:

"Please imagine a scenario where Wales could rejoin the European Union if it became an independent country. If a referendum was then held in Wales about becoming an independent country and this was the question, how would you vote? Should Wales be an independent country?"

Yes   39%   No   61%

	LAB	CON	PC	BREX	LD	Others
Yes	59%	11%	65%	22%	74%	22%
No	41%	89%	35%	78%	26%	78%

In this scenario, a majority (59 per cent) of people intending to vote Labour would vote in favour of independence, while 74 per cent of Liberal Democrat voters would. Overall, the 39 per cent who would vote Yes in this scenario is the highest figure reached by the hypothetical pro-independence campaign in any of the scenarios we tested, a result largely powered by the 58 per cent of 16 to 34-year-olds who would vote in favour.

Similar levels of support for independence were found when a second hypothetical question was asked in the April 2020 Survation poll:

"And now imagine a scenario where an independent Wales would be able to share significant political responsibilities with other nations across the British Isles – for example, on defence and foreign affairs. If a referendum was then held in Wales about becoming an independent country on this basis, how would you vote?"

Yes   38%   No   62%

	LAB	CON	PC	BREX	LD	Others
Yes	56%	13%	71%	22%	47%	9%
No	44%	87%	29%	78%	53%	91%

From a Plaid Cymru perspective, it is noteworthy that the highest level of support for independence among Plaid voters (71 per cent) is in response to this question. It suggests that there is strong support among those who vote for the party for an independent Wales seeking close collaboration with the other nations of Britain.

The constitutional preference question

A more nuanced perspective on support for independence is revealed when respondents are asked their views on a choice of future constitutional options for Wales, ranging from abolition of the Senedd to independence.

"Thinking about the National Assembly for Wales, which of these statements comes closest to your view?"

	Nov 2019 %	Jan 2020 %	June 2020 %
There should be no devolved government in Wales	17	17	22
The National Assembly for Wales / Welsh Parliament should have fewer powers	6	8	5
We should leave things as they are now	27	24	24
The National Assembly for Wales / Welsh Parliament should have more powers	21	18	20
Wales should become independent, separate from the UK	11	14	16
Don't Know / Refused / Won't Vote	18	19	14

On the constitutional preference question here, we find some modest growth in support for independence, albeit at a far lower level than a Yes/No question, with some apparent growth in support for the abolition of Welsh devolved government. On the other hand, there is substantial backing (36 per cent in June 2020) when support for the Senedd acquiring more powers is combined with support for independence.

Strength of feeling about independence

In November 2019 YouGov asked the following question:

"On a scale of 0 to 10, where 0 is very strongly against and 10 is very strongly in favour, how do you feel about Welsh independence?"

Anti-Independence (0-3)	48%
Indy-curious (4-6)	30%
Indy-confident (7-10)	23%

(12% of electors were Don't know or refused to answer and are excluded from this table)

In January and June 2020 YouGov asked a related but differently-worded question, this time on a scale of 0 to 100, where answers in the range of 0 to 39 were taken to signify the respondents were against independence, 40 to 69 Indy-curious, and 70 to 100 Indy-confident:

"People sometimes talk about how Wales is governed. On the scale shown below, where 0 means no devolution for Wales at all, and 100 means complete political independence for Wales, where would you place...**things as they are right now**?"

Which was followed up by:

"And where would you place... **how you would like to see Wales being governed**?"

The overall preferences are shown in the following table:

Individual preferences on independence	January 2020	June 2020
Anti-Independence (0-39)	35%	36%
Indy-curious (40-69)	32%	27%
Indy-confident (70-100)	33%	37%

Conclusions

This polling data suggest that, while a majority of the Welsh electorate does not favour Welsh independence today, a significant minority is well disposed towards the idea. The support increases further when placed in the context of what might be termed 'reassurance factors', for example rejoining the EU or British co-operation.

However, we lack more qualitative data as to what electors think in greater depth. Of those who are positively disposed towards, why do some voters report that they would support independence in a referendum, but given a wider range of constitutional options would opt for greater powers? What might persuade those who are currently Indy-curious to take a further step and become Indy-confident? What are the barriers to supporting Welsh independence? What are the concerns of those who are already supporting independence? Such questions could usefully be explored in focus groups to give a richer understanding of the data and provide researchers and politicians a broader basis upon which to draw conclusions on public attitudes. This suggests a role for the statutory National

Commission and associated Citizens' Assemblies recommended in this report.

CHAPTER 3

A Welsh jurisdiction

THE DEVOLUTION OF THE justice system and the establishment of a truly Welsh jurisdiction is central to creating a fair and independent Wales in which its governing institutions respond instinctively to the needs of its people. In the UK today, although there are three nations, one province and four legislatures, there are only three separate jurisdictions:

- Scotland
- Northern Ireland
- England **and** Wales

As Wales' experience of policy and law-making develop and Cardiff Bay grows in confidence, this historical jurisdictional structure must also develop to accommodate it. When he was Counsel General for Wales, Theodore Huckle QC commented:

"Across the Common Law world, the creation of new legislatures has been coupled with the formation of a distinct legal jurisdiction. But not in Wales."[9]

It is remarkable to consider that Wales is the only country in the world that has a legislature, but no legal jurisdiction of its own.

Asymmetric devolution

Debates surrounding the development of Wales as a separate jurisdiction have been impeded by the comparatively weak devolution settlement obtained by Wales, as compared with those of Northern Ireland and Scotland. The asymmetric devolution settlements in 1998 resulted in different levels of responsibility given to Wales, Scotland and Northern Ireland.

The Scottish Parliament and Executive have been able to pass Acts since 1998 and can make secondary legislation in all areas other than those reserved to Westminster.[10] The Northern Ireland Assembly also has the power to legislate in all areas which are not reserved to Westminster.[11]

By contrast, the Government of Wales Act 1998 only specified that certain areas should be devolved to the Welsh Assembly.[12] The Assembly was formed as a single corporate body with limited executive powers and no powers to enact primary legislation.[13] Since then, powers have been devolved incrementally (one might suggest, reluctantly). Powers were conferred to pass Measures and then Acts but only in specified and limited areas, under the Government of Wales Act 2006 and following the referendum of 2011.[14] Some tax-raising powers were transferred to the Assembly under the Wales Act 2014[15], and a reserved powers model, similar in concept to the Scotland system, was introduced under the Wales Act 2017.[16] The Senedd (that is, the newly-renamed Assembly) can now make laws on any matter except those reserved to the UK. One of those reserved matters is the single jurisdiction of England and Wales.[17]

This piecemeal devolution in Wales has resulted in an unnecessarily complex constitutional scheme which makes for poor accountability, ineffective delivery of justice policy, and inevitable confusion. Although Wales, Scotland and Northern Ireland can all now legislate in all areas that are not reserved to the UK Parliament under their respective devolution Acts, the powers reserved are still asymmetric. The fact that Scotland had its own legal system before devolution certainly played a part in ensuring its comparatively strong settlement.

We in Wales are still playing catch-up.

The single England and Wales jurisdiction

Wales became part of the English legal jurisdiction in the 1530s when Wales was incorporated into the realm of England. Until 1830 Wales retained a court system which differed somewhat from that in England. Thereafter, Wales's legal system was by and large the same as that of England until 1998 when the National Assembly for Wales was established. Hence, the well-known clichéd reference of the 1888 *Encyclopaedia Britannica* edition: 'For Wales, see England'.

Today, to a great extent, that perception persists. In the single England and Wales jurisdiction, Wales is seen very much as an appendage, and its, by now, distinct body of law is regarded by many in Whitehall as an irritating exception.

In contrast to Wales, Scotland retained its separate court structure, legal principles and legal system when it was united with England in 1707. The fact that in 1998 the legal administrative structure was already there to facilitate the process of legislating has streamlined Scottish devolution. To put it simply, the fact that Scotland has a separate legal structure has been a badge of nationhood that is missing for Wales.

Why Wales needs a separate jurisdiction

The burgeoning maturity of our justice system in Wales cannot be ignored. Certainly, there are few practical impediments to addressing this discrepancy between the different nations that make up the UK. After all Northern Ireland and Scotland operate successful systems without being tied to England.

In September 2017 the Commission on Justice in Wales was set up by the Labour Welsh Government to review the operation of the justice system in Wales and set a long-term vision for its future. Led by Lord Thomas of Cwmgiedd, a former Lord Chief Justice of England and Wales, it set out clearly why a distinct Welsh justice system and legal jurisdiction is needed. In summary:

"The fundamental problem lies in the split between two governments and two legislatures of responsibilities for justice on the one hand and social, health, education and economic development policies on the other.

This results in:
- An inability to allocate spending in a co-ordinated manner;
- A lack of accountability;
- A level of complexity which is wasteful of resources;
- Failure to develop and implement a coherent set of overall policies;
- A lack of innovation directed to the needs of the people of Wales; and
- Serious disadvantages to the people of Wales which people in England, Scotland and Northern Ireland do not experience."[18]

The report's detailed findings are compelling, incontrovertible and damning of the current justice system. As things stand, the people of Wales are being short-changed.

In their comprehensive 2018 volume, *Legislating for Wales*, Professor Thomas Watkin and Daniel Greenberg suggest three further, specific and fundamental findings that support the view that distinct jurisdictional arrangements are required in Wales:

"First, there is now developing **a distinct body of law**

which only applies to Wales, as there is also a distinct body of law which only applies to England. Both of those bodies of law will increase in size as divergent legislation is enacted in one or other country.

"Secondly, within the body of Welsh law are laws which have been enacted or made in both English and Welsh, with the result that, **by law, the two language versions must be treated as of equal standing** for all purposes. (GoWA 2006, section 156(1)). It is difficult to see how courts across England are meant to respond to this, or indeed why they should continue in theory to have to do so.

"Thirdly... under the Welsh Language Acts, parties before the courts in Wales – but not in neighbouring England – have **the right to be heard in either Welsh or English**. When trials are listed to be heard or moved outside of Wales for administrative convenience, this right is forfeit. The distinct right simply does not fit appropriately into the pre-existing single jurisdiction."[19]

The second of these issues was also addressed by the Law Commission in its report 'Form and Accessibility of the Law Applicable in Wales'. It endorsed the view that the interpretation of bilingual legislation requires, "that the exact meaning to be given to legislation depends on the meaning of both language texts" and that "this has implications... in that it requires proficiency in both languages to arrive at the meaning of the legislation."[20]

In short, the law which applies in Wales together with its judicial interpretation is different to that which applies in England, and the jurisdictional structure should reflect that reality.

In recent years, more and more people have joined the ranks of those calling for a just and comprehensive legal system fit for a modern Wales, including high-ranking members of the judiciary, senior academics, experts at the Wales Governance Centre at Cardiff University, and the Constitution Unit at University College London, the current Welsh Government and many more.

When the 2016 draft Wales Bill was being scrutinised by the Welsh Affairs Select Committee the majority of witnesses recommended that the diverging body of distinct Welsh law could be best served only by a distinct jurisdiction.[21] Lawyers and constitutional experts alike reiterated the case that to establish a clear and lasting legal settlement for Wales a distinct legal jurisdiction is necessary. Constitutional expert Professor Richard Wyn Jones summarised this in a pithy and memorable phrase – a Welsh jurisdiction represents "the constitution catching up with the legislative reality".[22]

The report of the Commission on Justice in Wales states unequivocally:

"Under the current scheme of devolution there is no properly joined up or integrated approach, as justice remains controlled by the Westminster Government. Consequently, **the people of Wales do not have the benefit which the people of Scotland, Northern Ireland and England enjoy by justice being an integral part of overall policy making**. There is no rational basis for Wales to be treated differently, particularly as Wales has its own long legal tradition."[23]

And again:

"**The people of Wales both need and deserve a better system**. Justice is not an island and should be truly integrated into policies for a just, fair and prosperous Wales."[24]

A virtual legal jurisdiction

The criteria usually employed to define a separate jurisdiction is that it should:

- Operate in a defined territory;
- Have a distinct body of law; and
- Be supported by its own court structure and legal institutions.

Wales has been a defined territory under the law of England and Wales since the passing of the Sunday Closing (Wales) Act 1881 which applied solely to the 'principality of Wales'.[25] Since then, Westminster has enacted several statutes that have pertained only to Wales as a self-contained territory, such as the Welsh Church Act 1914 and the Welsh Language Acts of 1967 and 1993. The Local Government Act 1972, though not a Wales-only statute, contained separate provisions for both England and Wales in separate Parts of the Act, and thus, in its content and structure, reinforced the concept of Wales as a legally defined territory, distinct from England.

Wales also has a distinct and growing body of law. Since primary law-making powers were devolved to the Welsh Assembly in 2006, the body of Welsh law has grown and diverged from that of England. Lawyers who practise environmental, criminal, family and, of course, administrative law must have a thorough knowledge of the corpus of Welsh law if they are to practise in Wales.

In these terms Wales already has its own jurisdiction, since the 'distinct body of law' passed by the Senedd in Cardiff pertains only to the 'defined territory' of Wales. As Professor Thomas Watkin put it in his evidence to the Justice Commission:

"... in terms of its laws, Wales is no longer the same as England; one can no longer say, 'For Wales, see England'."[26]

Nonetheless, Wales remains part of the single jurisdiction of England and Wales. The process now needs to be completed. The developing corpus of Welsh law and the inevitably divergent paths of public policy in Wales and England need to be supported by Wales's 'own court structure and legal institutions'.

Justice powers

A separate Welsh jurisdiction is a central building block on the road to independence. But the establishment of a Welsh jurisdiction is not predicated on an independent Wales. Independence would lead naturally to the creation of a Welsh jurisdiction, but a Welsh jurisdiction could certainly be established without independence.

To secure a distinct Welsh jurisdiction Wales needs to have full legislative powers over all justice matters. Under the Wales Act 2017, the single jurisdiction of England and Wales is a matter reserved to the UK Parliament and lies outside the remit of the Senedd in Cardiff. The Commission on Justice in Wales states:

"Only full legislative devolution, combined with executive powers, will overcome the obstacles of the current devolution scheme."[27]

The setting up of a separate jurisdiction would follow quite naturally after justice in its entirety is devolved. A truly distinct jurisdiction would be possible, an integrated system of policy and execution responding to the needs of the people of Wales.

Despite the growing consensus and the compelling arguments for a separate Welsh jurisdiction, the current UK Government has shown no interest in revisiting the current settlement. A concerted campaign of persuasion is needed.

Implications of a distinct Welsh jurisdiction

Disentangling the current single England and Wales jurisdictional scheme gives rise to a number of issues.

1. What kind of jurisdiction?

Wales has an opportunity to tailor a justice system which is appropriate for the country, its people and its specific character. The creation of a Welsh jurisdiction on a blank canvas opens up exciting and imaginative possibilities. What kind of justice system should Wales adopt? For example, would an independent Wales opt for an investigative or an adversarial system? As Lord Thomas of Cwmgiedd said when he addressed the Legal Wales Conference in 2013:

> "There is no reason why [Wales] cannot develop its own innovative style... Westminster is burdened by history. It is therefore a model that does not have to be followed."[28]

2. Common law

The establishment of a separate Welsh legal jurisdiction would have an impact on the common law that has evolved over centuries under the unified jurisdiction of England and Wales. Separate laws and jurisdictions, together with the different social and cultural backgrounds and the divergence in policies of the two nations, would mean that the context in which the evolution takes place would differ as between Wales and England. This must be seen as a positive development.

3. Learning from elsewhere

A Welsh jurisdiction would not necessarily seek to isolate itself from the prevailing jurisprudences in other jurisdictions. For example, in the area of the laws of tort in England and Wales the courts have frequently looked at Canadian, Australian and New Zealand authorities as well as to other common law jurisdictions. These references often created the laws of tort as they currently apply in England and Wales. Consideration of what is happening in other jurisdictions is another positive development.

4. Implications for the professions and cross-border considerations

A consensus would have to be reached as to whether a separate jurisdiction would require a distinctly Welsh qualification for practitioners in Wales. The Thomas Commission suggests that this is unnecessary and recommends that the present system should be continued.[29] Inevitably, if it was decided to create a separate legal profession for Wales, there would also be implications for cross-border practitioners.

In Northern Ireland, arrangements for qualification and rights of audience are separate and there is no automatic right to practise in England and Wales (the same applies in the opposite direction). Those wishing to work in another jurisdiction can make arrangements and comply with requirements set down by professional bodies. There are simplified arrangements available for barristers who are conducting a specific case or cases in another jurisdiction, rather than those looking to practise there on an ongoing basis. Those who wish to undertake work at the bar in Northern Ireland but who are qualified as a barrister in England and Wales need only complete some forms and pay a fee for the temporary right of audience within the jurisdiction of Northern Ireland.

Scotland, having had its own jurisdiction for centuries, is different. The process of qualification to practise within the Scottish jurisdiction is considerable. In Scotland qualified lawyer transfer tests, or QLTTs, are used as intra-UK transfer tests. The more demanding qualification process probably reflects the huge divergence in law and practice in Scotland from that which pertains in England and Wales. The tests are held twice yearly in May and November, though only small numbers tend to sit them. Once this test has been passed, lawyers can apply to become a solicitor in Scotland on a permanent basis.

After independence the current jointly regulated system for legal practitioners in England and Wales would cease to exist, since the notion of a unified legal profession across both nations would become unsustainable and otiose.

5. The judiciary, the court structure, and the UK Supreme Court

A Welsh jurisdiction could have whatever structures and institutions it was decided best served the interests of Wales. There is no template which has to be followed, and once created, a jurisdiction is not immutable. It can change and develop as needs dictate. The present Northern Ireland jurisdiction is, for example, structurally different from the one that was originally established.

The Thomas Commission recommends that, when legislative responsibility of the justice system has been devolved, the Senedd should establish a separate judiciary in Wales involving a High Court and a Court of Appeal.[30] A Welsh Courts and Tribunals Service should be established, merging the courts and tribunals into a single structure, organised on the same basis as courts and tribunals in Scotland.[31] It also recommends that the UK Supreme Court should remain as an emerging Constitutional Court and that Wales should have equality with Scotland and Northern Ireland as regards the appointment of judges to the Supreme Court.[32]

As a first step, such a system could and should be established prior to independence.

On independence, there would be opportunities to innovate to respond to the needs of the Welsh people. The continuing relevance of the UK Supreme Court would depend on the constitutional arrangements that had been established between the independent nations of Britain.

6. Cost

The budget for the England and Wales Ministry of Justice budget was cut by 27 per cent between 2011 and 2018, which had a significant impact in Wales.[33] Westminster's annual spend on the justice system in England and Wales in 2017-2018 was around £376 per head. The equivalent figures in Scotland and Northern Ireland were £560 and £666. If we were to rely on a transfer of funds based on these calculations, Wales would be handed 'a poisoned chalice' – run-down services and an inadequate level of resources to fund them.[34]

Unsurprisingly, this meagre funding has had to be supplemented in order to mitigate the most damaging effects of Westminster's austerity policy. Wales now contributes almost 40 per cent of the justice spend in Wales from its own very limited financial resources. This is unsustainable when most of the justice system is still a reserved matter and the Welsh Government and Senedd have so little say in justice policy and overall spending.[35]

The way ahead

In its report, *Justice in Wales for the People of Wales*, the Commission listed 78 recommendations. under ten different headings:

- Information, advice and assistance.
- Criminal justice.
- Civil justice.
- Administrative justice and coroners.
- Family justice.

- Delivering justice: locality and structure.
- The legal sector and the economy of Wales.
- Knowledge, skills and innovation.
- The Welsh language.
- Governance, the law of Wales and the judiciary.

Most importantly the Commission insisted that:

"… the lack of clear and accountable leadership in the field of justice has had an adverse impact on Wales. … There need to be clear lines of accountability for justice within the Welsh Government."[36]

A cohesive approach under dynamic leadership is needed.

The Thomas Commission has set out its recommendations clearly and concisely. Most of them are uncontroversial and eminently adoptable. It has signposted what can be done immediately, what can be done under the present devolution scheme with the co-operation of Westminster, and what can be done with legislative devolution. The Commission's final recommendation is:

"The Welsh Government should begin the process of reform by listing the recommendations it will seek to implement while the current scheme of devolution continues. The Assembly should make arrangements to monitor and review the process of reform."[37]

Currently, all justice matters in Wales are the responsibility of the Counsel General, the Government's chief legal adviser and representative in the courts. The current Counsel General is also the Minister for European Transition. He carries a heavy portfolio. We recommend that an incoming Plaid Government should immediately create a single ministerial portfolio, separate from that of the Counsel General, bringing together the diverse and unco-ordinated justice functions currently held by the Welsh Government. This would:

- Enable the development of a coherent overview of all aspects of the justice and legal system in Wales which would then inform and reflect the Government's strategy and policies.
- Provide clear accountability for the justice policies which lie within the competence of the Welsh Government.
- Provide impetus to the codification and accessibility of the law in Wales under the Legislation (Wales) Act 2019.
- Enable the Government to lead, in co-operation with the judiciary, the professions and the law schools, on work to invigorate the legal system in Wales and to raise awareness of Welsh law within Wales.
- Provide leadership on a programme to implement the Thomas Commission's recommendations where possible under the current devolution scheme.
- Ensure the focus needed for progressing the evolvement of a distinct Welsh jurisdiction.

These would be only the first steps towards realising a separate Welsh jurisdiction and a justice system responsive to the needs of the Welsh people. But they are steps that can be taken now. A pro-active Plaid Government in 2021 should lay the groundwork in anticipation of legislative devolution and eventually an independent Wales. It should inspire all who practise in the field of justice in Wales to work together to promote a progressive, integrated, sustainable and truly just system. As Lord Thomas of Cwmgiedd and his Commission stated:

"We have unanimously concluded that the people of Wales are being let down by the system in its current state."[38]

There is an urgent need for change. Justice should be at the heart of government, underpinning all policies and legislation. Working towards a Welsh jurisdiction and justice system that is fit, fair and accessible to all the people of Wales should be a priority for a Welsh Government.

Recommendations

1. Wales is developing its own body of laws and should have a separate jurisdiction.

2. The Welsh Government should begin the process of reform, leading to a separate Welsh jurisdiction. This can be put into effect while the current scheme of devolution continues by implementing the Commission on Justice for Wales's recommendations. However, the reservation to Westminster of powers relating to the single jurisdiction needs to be removed.

3. Arrangements should be made for the Senedd to monitor and review the process of reform.

4. A single portfolio, a Minister for Justice separate from that of the Counsel General, should be created, bringing together the diverse and unco-ordinated justice functions currently held by the Welsh Government.

5. The Minister of Justice should set out a pathway for implementation and take a leadership role across all sectors in driving forward the Commission on Justice in Wales' recommendations for creating a separate Welsh legal jurisdiction.

CHAPTER 4

Effective Government and the civil service

THE CIVIL SERVICE CONSTITUTES a substantial part of the executive machinery of government and is consequently a fundamental part of any state's constitution. Depending on its structure, leadership and underlying culture it can be a powerful driver of change, but equally it can be a powerful inhibitor of change. In the 2020s the role, leadership and motivation of the Welsh civil service will be an important determinant of progress towards independence. Inevitably, given that the civil service is reserved to Westminster, its starting position will be an outlook that regards an integrated England and Wales civil service as part of the glue that holds the United Kingdom together.

During the first twenty years of devolution the Welsh civil service has grown significantly in size, and has adapted to many changes, especially arising from the acquisition of new legislative and financial powers following on from the 2011 referendum. However, its underlying culture arising from close ties between the wider England and Wales civil service has, in all essentials, remained unaltered.

Notably, the civil service culture in Scotland has developed along a different path. This is partly because the Scottish Parliament inherited an already more autonomous civil service that served the former Scottish Office. More recently, it is because of the political change that occurred as a result of the 2007 election and the policies of SNP Governments that have been in power since that time.

In Wales, the National Assembly inherited a civil service that had developed within the Welsh Office. Compared with the Scottish Office, founded in 1880, the Welsh Office was only established in 1964, and was far more integrated with Whitehall policies and direction. Moreover, Scotland's separate legal jurisdiction gave it a freer hand.

Since the beginning of political devolution, the Welsh Government has been run either by Labour Governments or Labour-led coalition Governments – with the Liberal Democrats (2000-2003) and Plaid Cymru (2007-2011). Such a long period of, in effect, one-party rule remains unsurpassed in most democratic cultures.

All this will present the Welsh civil service with significant challenges when faced with a Plaid Cymru Government in May 2021. Not only will it be required to adopt markedly different policy directions in such fields as health, education, and the economy, but it will also be charged with preparing the ground for an independence referendum.

Twenty years of evolution

When the National Assembly was first elected, the number of civil servants it inherited from the Welsh Office was just under 3,000. A year before the first Assembly election in 1999 the Welsh Office Permanent Secretary Rachel Lomax made clear her view that the advent of democratic devolution implied fundamental change. Civil servants were going to have to get used to the democratic glare of publicity:

"Believe me, a department that answers to sixty politicians

who in turn answer to the people from all over Wales, is going to respond very differently from one that answers to one Cabinet Minister, whoever he or she is… We are going to have to get used to explaining ourselves in public."[39]

Rhodri Morgan, who became First Minister in early 2000, acted on Rachel Lomax's interpretation. By 2003, at the end of the Assembly's first term, the size of the Welsh civil service had increased by about 30 per cent to a little under 4,000. During this period there was a separation between 300 civil servants who served the Presiding Office and the rest who served the government. This *de facto* distinction between the legislature and the executive was made *de jure* by the 2006 Government of Wales Act which also transferred the beginnings of primary legislative powers to the Assembly.

By the time it acquired full legislative powers, as a result of the 2011 referendum, the size of the Welsh civil service had grown close to 6,000. This was partly due to its absorption of the Welsh Development Agency, Education and Learning Wales (ELWa), and the Wales Tourist Board. These mergers brought into the civil service people with an operational and service delivery background that sometimes clashed with the more traditional administrative and policy-related culture they encountered. As one highly-placed official involved in the mergers at the time, recalled some years later:

"I well remember the battles between traditional civil servants and ex-Quango staff when we wanted to get things done. By now, of course, ex-Quango staff have moved on and the traditionalists have all but taken over."[40]

The acquisition of primary legislative powers as a result of the 2011 referendum, and some tax-raising powers following the

2014 Wales Act, required a good deal of internal administrative innovation. The Office of the Legislative Counsel acquired greater scope and independence. It had first been established in 2007 to deal with the drafting of Legislative Competence Orders and primary legislation in the form of Assembly Measures under the 2006 Government of Wales Act. The Welsh Treasury and Welsh Revenue Authority were created in 2015 to deal with the emerging new fiscal and taxation powers.

In 2007 seven Director Generals had been appointed to operate immediately below the Permanent Secretary to bring greater co-ordination to the administration. Attempts were also made to strengthen a central policy role with the establishment of the Delivery Unit in 2011. Later this became the Office of the First Minister and Cabinet.

Despite these developments the numbers of civil servants fell back to a little over 5,000 by 2012, a reduction dictated by the Westminster Government's austerity programme.[41] Partly because of this, in 2015, the Director Generals were reduced from seven to four and made responsible for:

- Office of First Minister and Cabinet (Europe and Brexit, Legislation and Legal Services, Constitutional Affairs, International Relations, Social Partnerships).
- Health and Social Services.
- Education and Public Services.
- Economy, Skills and Natural Resources.

Despite all these changes since 1999, the operation and culture of the Welsh civil service has not altered fundamentally. It inherited a Whitehall approach to governance which has remained remarkably the same. At the outset of devolution twenty years ago it adopted an ineffectual Whitehall model of administration in the form of the Welsh Office. In those days the tendency was for the Welsh Office to do what England did, but six months later. By and large, its civil servants lacked a tradition of intellectual inquiry or the confidence that prompts exploration of distinctive policy options. This has been acquired slowly over the past 20 years, but often with reluctance and certainly not at pace.

The contrast with the Scottish Office is instructive. It was a more powerful department, more autonomous, and with greater clout in Whitehall. Its civil servants maintained and enhanced that tradition when they moved to serving the Scottish Government, and especially after 2007 when the SNP took control. As former First Minister Rhodri Morgan put it:

> "In the Scottish Office which had been around for 100 years they had developed a tradition of independent policy. The Welsh Office had no capability of policy-making at all until the late 1960s. Likewise you promoted staff in the Scottish Office on the basis that they had put one over on Whitehall. You promoted staff in the Welsh Office on the basis of whether they had kept their nose clean in Whitehall."[42]

Of course, the Scottish Office had a much longer history than its Welsh counterpart and was built on very different civic foundations that were not part of the Welsh experience. In particular, Scotland's separate legal system and jurisdiction had survived the 1707 parliamentary union with England.

The civil service culture

Welsh Government civil servants are part of the British Home Civil Service which is led by the Prime Minister and the Head of the Civil Service. Consequently, the appointment process for the Welsh Permanent Secretary is managed by the Whitehall Cabinet Office and approved by the Civil Service Commission. Until 2012 final approval came from the Prime Minister. However, that role has now been delegated to the Head of the Civil Service.

The First Minister has a role in drawing up a shortlist for the appointment. But at the end of the day he or she cannot choose but only refuse. The Permanent Secretary from the London Cabinet Office chairs the process that includes one or two non-executive Directors from the Welsh Government Management Board. Essentially, however, it is a London appointment. The First Minister sits alongside the process rather than being part of it. In short, the choice is made according to Whitehall criteria. That judgement will not necessarily bear on whether the person is the best choice for Wales.

Any civil service is inevitably a bureaucracy, and there is an inbuilt tendency for bureaucracies to be cautious, risk-averse, and focused on compliance rather than action. There is evidence, from the observations of a number of commentators, that the Welsh civil service is particularly prone to these characteristics. One close observer, former Vice Chancellor of the University of South Wales Sir Adrian Webb, for ten years a non-executive director on the Welsh Government's Management Board, chaired by the Permanent Secretary, reported:

> "Welsh Government is too often very slow. Outside organisations are routinely frustrated by the lack of pace. This is inevitably true of government when viewed from a non-public organization – government has to cover bases which others do not. But there is good reason to believe that Wales is often especially slow. I have worked with a number of Whitehall civil servants who find the context in Wales unbelievably frustrating."[43]

Webb identifies the core problem as being a failure of delivery. He argues the Welsh Government operates on a 'management model' rather than a 'leadership of joined-up delivery model', driven by a sense of urgency:

"The current mindset puts delivery second best to maintenance of the status quo – especially in the layers of the civil service just below the top. While many civil servants do seek to deliver, civil servants are simply not held *systematically accountable* for delivery or for acting with a sense of urgency."[44]

From his direct experience, Webb reports that this 'mindset' operates from the top of the Welsh civil service machine. For example, he had been involved in UK Cabinet Office "appraisals of successive Permanent Secretaries for salary purposes". Yet: "At no time was delivery against specified goals a consideration."[45]

Webb writes that there is a confusion in the Welsh civil service between delivery, which is associated with activity and the avoidance of error, and measurable outcomes:

"There tends to a box ticking drive to ensure Manifesto and Programme promises can be said to have been met. What I have never seen is an overall attempt to assess whether the desired *outcomes* underlying the Programme for Government and the Manifesto are being advanced. I was a member of the Board for nearly 10 years and I have never been part of a Board with such a lack of measures of progress or outcome success. *The only data routinely seen by the board are budgetary.* Parts of the system do try to use outcome and performance measures, but this meets considerable resistance from some civil servants. The fact that metrics are resisted tells its own tale."[46]

Another close observer is Graeme Guilford, former senior manager with Amersham International, a member of the EU Wales Structural Funds Monitoring Committee and currently a member of the Welsh Government's Regional Investment for

Wales Steering Group. His assessment supports Adrian Webb's judgement about the lack of a 'delivery culture' inside the Welsh Government. Discussing the lessons that need to be learned from the past in order to design a post-Brexit regional development policy, he reflected:

"This focus on delivery is largely absent within the Structural Funds area. In my experience this is mainly because there has been an assumption that delivery is something that simply 'happens' once the project is approved. Indeed, for many projects funding was approved before a project delivery team was in place or even recruited. Within much of the public sector in Wales, project management is seen as a relatively junior administrative function rather than the key, make or break role it occupies in the private sector. This means that the 'heroes' in the process are the people who write the successful project application not the people who successfully deliver the project. This lack of focus on delivery was exacerbated by the absence of an effective central support system to help struggling projects particularly in their early stages."[47]

Professor Gerry Holtham had a close-up view of the operation of the Welsh civil service when he acted as Special Adviser to Finance Minister Jane Hutt for three years between 2012 and 2014. In 2019 he reported a lack of a collective decision-making culture in which priorities were shared across departments:

"Instead, departments have acted like semi-independent fiefdoms where the Minister had a policy, which he or she had considerable latitude to change without much Cabinet discussion. Indeed, one Minister was reputed to have never brought a policy paper to Cabinet in a long ministerial career… Such ministerial quasi-independence leads to silo-thinking. Moreover, it limits the ability of the government more generally to think strategically and reflect that in budgetary allocations. In the past, the usual practice has been for every department's budget to go up (or down) by a standard amount. The exception, invariably, has been for looming crises in the health service to require extra money and a consequent haircut for other policy areas… The lack of overarching priorities in government has bedevilled work across departments at the official level as well. Meetings involving officials from several departments have operated in slow motion. Because the work was not the 'baby' of their own Minister it was fitted in by civil servants in other departments with all the other calls on their time. The next meeting was always scheduled on the first day that everyone said they could attend given their other diary commitments. When priorities are uncertain, the diary rules. This means that cross-departmental work proceeds sluggishly. Where differences have not been thrashed out at Cabinet level, inter-departmental meetings called to implement decisions tend to reflect different degrees of enthusiasm between them. The result is that, rather than working for a common purpose, civil servants are engaged in a perpetual negotiation This is debilitating and bad for morale."[48]

In an earlier paper Holtham identified the cause of these and other problems around civil service delivery as being a lack of a strong co-ordinating hand at the centre of the Welsh Government. Indeed, he said Wales had a 'Polo-mint' government, one with a hole in the middle:

"There is no substantial First Minister's department, no

strong Cabinet Office and no real Treasury in the Welsh government. There is no body that is supposed to help frame an overall strategy or to co-ordinate the strategies of different ministries, which all too often operate with detached independence. If the First Minister wants to create an industrial strategy driving the infrastructure plan and to ensure that the policies of all departments are in harmony with it, he will have his work cut out. The institutions to help him are not there. You won't get joined up government if a chunk of the government's central nervous system is missing."[49]

A Welsh public service

Wales is both small and large enough for its public sector organisations to collaborate more closely, so the whole can be greater than the sum of its parts. The way forward is to reduce the barriers between those working in different parts of the public sector – the Welsh Government, health authorities, local government, sponsored bodies, university administration, and so on. We need a shared Welsh public service to make this change. Lowering the barriers would result in broader career opportunities, greater understanding between sectors, and the creation of a set of shared values around pursuing what is best for Wales. It would instil a delivery culture across the public services, in which implementation would be a priority alongside administration and policy development.

Arguments for this approach were made in the early years of the Welsh Government, but they were never taken up in a way that would result in systemic change. For instance, the case for a Welsh public service was made by First Minister Rhodri Morgan, in a speech he delivered in 2002:

"We need to invent a new form of public service in Wales, in which individuals are able to move far more easily than now between one form of organisation and another. Local government employees, Assembly civil servants, health service administrators, and staff from the Assembly Sponsored Public Bodies should all be able to map out career paths which move between these bodies, developing expertise and cross-fertilising from one place to another... When I visited Australia earlier in the autumn, the top educational civil servant in the state had been a professor of education and had entered the government service from being the Vice-Chancellor of the local university – and had moved into academic life from a career in public administration. Zig-zagging your way up the promotional ladder in civil service and academic terms seems entirely healthy to me and particularly suitable to post-devolution Wales. It is completely consistent with the principle of innovation rather than imitation. We need a Welsh public service, rather than a Welsh civil service... I am drawing attention not simply to the advantages of a new flexibility in the way in which individuals can flow between academic and public careers, but also to the intellectual power which our higher education institutions are able to mobilise, and which I wish to see better harnessed to the benefit of the citizens of Wales."[50]

These views were endorsed across a broad political spectrum, for example by Plaid Cymru in its evidence to the Richard Commission in 2003:

"An integrated public service would include public servants working for local authorities and other public bodies, including the health service and ASPBs, as well as the

Assembly's own civil servants. This would make possible the creation of career paths for public servants within Wales, broader experience of government at all levels, and strengthen mutual understanding between those levels. It would entail the establishment of a National Public Service College. This development would open up opportunities for exchanges with public/civil services in the different nations and regions of Britain, as well as secondments/exchanges with the European Commission and indeed administrations in other European nations and regions."[51]

Such recommendations were considered too radical. Instead, a Public Sector Management Initiative (PSMI), organised from within the civil service, was established. Its role, as explained by Permanent Secretary Sir Jon Shortridge, was to secure:

"… common leadership and management training for staff working in all parts of the public sector in Wales – the Assembly civil service, the National Health Service, Local Authorities, Sponsored Bodies, and other Civil Service Departments. This should mean that over time Wales will develop its own cadre of public servants with experience in and understanding of different parts of the public sector in Wales. They should also have an established network of contacts in different parts of the Welsh public sector. This, coupled with the policy on open recruitment, should mean that there will increasingly be a common set of values and experiences among staff in the Welsh public sector. This in turn should help to reduce the frictions that currently exist within the policy 'delivery chain', and at the same time broaden and enhance the career opportunities for those people wishing to pursue a public sector career in Wales."[52]

The PSMI set about arranging courses and 'away day' events for senior managers across the Welsh public sector. In 2011 PSMI changed its name and organisation to Academi Wales, a virtual (mainly on-line) training college offering a variety of courses, including a Master's in Leadership and Governance. Its website commits to 'One Welsh Public Service' whose mission is to produce:

"... a fundamental shift toward more empowered citizens and communities and a more enabling state... We need to create a culture that cuts across organisational boundaries and sectors. Where everyone involved in the delivery of public services in Wales is part of this common endeavour, sharing common values and working together for the benefit of the people of Wales."[53]

However, we believe Academi Wales is not fit for purpose to deliver these aspirations. Its latest annual report, for 2018-19, says that it delivered 400 events, workshops, courses and conferences during the year at a cost of £1.2million. It has an Advisory Board drawn from local government, universities, health boards, community housing, and the voluntary sector – but not from the Welsh Government itself.[54]

There is little sense that Academi Wales is a central Welsh Government concern. If it was it would have a bigger budget and the Permanent Secretary would have a role in delivering its vision. As it is, Academi Wales has a low profile, and even lower impact. Certainly, it is not engaged in organising secondments across the Welsh public sector.

Of course, within the context of the present unified UK 'Home Civil Service' it would be difficult to create a meaningful 'Welsh public service' with a single cadre of people, sharing common grades and remuneration across a wide range of organisations.

Nevertheless, if there was a will Wales could set on a path in this direction.

For example, there could be more movement between the Welsh Government civil service and other parts of the public service in Wales, through secondment. However, at present civil service practice militates against this happening. If a civil servant is outsourced this is regarded as a backward career step. There is no guarantee they will resume their civil service career at the same level or with the same prospects of promotion when they return. This culture could be altered if it was made clear that secondment to other parts of the public sector in Wales was a positive career move, to gain experience, and that an equivalent position when the secondment was completed was guaranteed. But this would require leadership from the top.

Recommendations

1. The appointment of the Welsh Permanent Secretary should be made by the First Minister of Wales on the advice of an independent Welsh Civil Service Commission.

2. Within the Cabinet there should be a more collective and cohesive decision-making process, over the setting of the budget and cross-departmental working. This should entail putting in place a strategic delivery plan for the Programme of Government, with an agreed annual timetable and targets across the five-year term.

3. The Finance Department should take on a greater Treasury role and, working closely with the First Minister's Office, deliver greater co-ordination of policy delivery according to targets across the whole of the Welsh Government.

4. A central Policy Unit should be set up within the First Minister's Office to work on strategic questions and ensure delivery across departments.

5.   The role of the senior civil service should be re-defined as that of leading change that will benefit Wales – rather than managing the machine and protecting the status quo.

6.   Welsh Government should develop proposals and a timetable for the creation of a Public Service for Wales, with a shared culture, grades and pay scales across all public sector organisations, including the Welsh Government's civil service. This would require that the reservation to Westminster of powers relating to the civil service be removed.

7.   Welsh Government's Academi Wales should become a National School of Public Management and Governance, attached to the Welsh university sector. It should have an increased budget, a Board of Directors to include the Permanent Secretary and an independent Chair. It should develop an international research programme related to small country governance and enter into partnership arrangements with other management schools such as the Kennedy School of Government at Harvard and Insead.

CHAPTER 5

Addressing the fiscal gap

C AN WALES AFFORD INDEPENDENCE? Is Wales simply too poor? These questions are understandably raised when the case for such a step is made. Of course, in practice any country can afford to be independent, but the key question is whether it would be better or worse off compared with the status quo. Analyses by Wales Fiscal Analysis and the ONS shed light on the current fiscal position of Wales but reflect the current constitutional arrangements where Wales is not an independent state, but a region subordinated to the interests of London and the south east of England. As such it is subject to the fiscal policies determined by the UK Government. Under the current constitutional arrangements in 2018-19 it was estimated that Wales had a deficit of roughly 18 per cent of GDP or £4,300 per person.

Only three of Britain's 12 planning regions – London, the South East and East of England –are net contributors to the UK budget. However, the gap between what is raised in revenue in Wales and what is spent on public services is higher than in all but one region. The average is a much more modest £620 per head. So, is our best bet just to plough on and hope we can narrow the gap and reduce this amount over time?

Indeed, do we not need this security to deal with the damaging consequences of the coronavirus pandemic, the effects of which are likely to be felt strongly in territories such as Wales? Moreover, Wales is deficient in those sectors which have a greater share of the digital and other industries that are likely to benefit as a result of changes due to the pandemic, and more dependent on others, such as tourism, that will be hardest hit. The consequences and costs of coronavirus will unfold over many years to come. Would not Wales be better off in a union with the rest of Britain as it adjusts to harsh new realities across the economy and society?

For all that it has bright spots, the Welsh economy has chronic structural weaknesses that have proved hard to overcome for a long time. They include industry structure, external ownership and management, low productivity, a missing middle of medium-sized companies, vulnerability to takeover, a low export propensity, and educational and skills shortcomings. All have combined with poor road, rail and telecommunications infrastructure to leave Wales among the poorest UK economic regions and stymied attempts to raise its relative position.

Better, it might be argued, to take the money and rely on a subsidy that enables Welsh people to enjoy household incomes and living standards broadly the same as those of the rest of the UK. Un-supplemented revenues raised in Wales would be enough to pay for the public services offered in Portugal – a much poorer country. Instead, we have roughly the same services as Ireland, a richer country on most measures. Many will argue this is a trade-off too valuable to lose.

Is this the way we want to go on? Do the present arrangements offer a serious prospect of improving our economic and social well-being and reducing the Welsh fiscal gap over time? Could our dependence even be a consequence of continued reliance on subsidy?

The unvarnished truth is that Wales has been sliding backwards in relation to the richer regions of the United Kingdom, and especially London and the South East, for the past 50 years. All pretence that the gap could be closed or even significantly narrowed has now been buried in suggested new formulations of how prosperity should be measured.

This is too seductive. 'Well-being' and other similar measurement concepts designed to look at society's health and wealth, other than through the prism of more recognised gauges of wealth, are important. They should not be put up, however, as a way of avoiding problems of poor economic performance and entrenched poverty across a broad section of the population.

Population growth offers one telling proxy for Wales's relative decline. After a sharp decrease in the 1920s because of outward migration, numbers stood at 2.59 million in 1931 and rose only by 3,000 in the next 20 years. By contrast Scotland's population grew by 253,415 to 5.095m in 1951, while England recorded an increase of 3.7m to 41.147m. What has happened since, however, is equally interesting. England's population has risen by 37 per cent to 56.29m, Wales's by 23 per cent to 3.2m and Scotland's by an even more modest 7 per cent to 5.46m.

Wales is now down to 4.9 per cent of Britain's population, from 5.3 per cent after the war. Scotland has fallen from 10.4 per cent to 8.4 per cent. Meanwhile, England is three percentage points higher at 87 per cent. If the population of Wales had climbed at the same rate as that of England there would now be 3.56m people living in the country – half a million more. Each of these missing individuals represents a loss, or a potential loss, of employees, output, and creativity.

Would a break with the status quo make sense, therefore, and could it set Wales on a new trajectory that does not presage, as our present does, continued marginalisation within these isles? Could the cold turkey of coming off subsidy be a stimulus to the creation of a new Wales, one confidently able, albeit after a period of adjustment, to join the comity of nations? Other nations with similar numbers prosper, Indeed, a population of five million, or roughly half as much again as Wales, seems a near optimum – as in Denmark, Ireland, and New Zealand.

As the Covid-19 crisis has shown, in terms of managing the spread of the virus these countries have done better than such scientific powerhouses as Britain and the United States. In this crisis, strong and consistent political leadership, and good on-the-ground public health systems, have been as important in managing the outbreak as world-leading epidemiologists, virologists, medical researchers, statisticians, and disease modellers.

In other areas, too, small nations can be nimble, and can try different approaches. In an age when territorial aggrandisement is no longer the threat it once was, the defence advantages of being part of a bigger unit are less important. Indeed, the costs of trying to stay at the top table of military powers can be crippling, as the old Soviet Union found.

Trade, too, is now largely under multinational rules, making it more difficult for small nations to be bullied by their bigger neighbours when disputes occur. As the economist John Kay has pointed out:

"...there are few economies of scale in statehood. Size is as much a disadvantage as an advantage when it comes to carrying out the principal functions of modern government: justice, health, education, internal security."[55]

Even so, a hard question for proponents of independence to counter is that in the past 20 years, Wales has had more control than ever previously over its economy, transport, health and education systems and has hardly made a good fist of it. Would a step further into the unknown be sensible? Where will the capacity to make the transformational improvements come from?

It can be argued that it is precisely because we are trapped within an economy overwhelmingly shaped in the interests of the

City of London that Wales has failed to make economic progress. Fiscal analyses of the position of Wales as an economic region of the UK reflects the result of its past and current status within the British state: a 'region' subject to economic policies formulated to serve the interests of the City of London and the South East of England. The very fact that nine of the 12 countries and regions of the UK are persistently in deficit is an indication of the broken fiscal and economic model. It is a model that simply has not and does not deliver prosperity to Wales and offers no expectation of doing so in the future.

A better model

During the past 20 years the Labour Welsh Government's frequently updated plans for boosting the economy have failed to produce the step changes needed in performance. Initiative weariness is being manifested. Leading economists and others have started to ask the independence question: might a new constitutional settlement with the rest of Great Britain deliver the desired results?

In an article in early 2020 Professor Mark Barry of Cardiff University rejected the idea that Wales might be too poor or too small to be independent. If it were true, he said, Wales would be unique globally, the only place where an independent country of three million people could not exist. The question was could our economy and well-being be best served by Westminster and Whitehall, or by something more radical and more common across the world?[56]

How the economy of a successful, independent Wales might function is a challenge for the future. Some clues might be taken from the report of the Sustainable Growth Commission chaired by former member of the Scottish Parliament, Andrew Wilson, which reported to the SNP Government in Edinburgh in 2018. It argued that Scotland has an economic potential that far outstrips its current longer-term performance, and that the ambition for the country should be to perform to the level of the best of the small advanced economies.

The report argues that a centralised 'big country' model which concentrates too much economic activity in London and the South East region is holding Scotland and the other regions and nations of the UK below their potential. A similar point is made in a separate report by the UK2070 Commission under the chairmanship of Lord Kerslake, a former head of the civil service. It observed that 50 years of effort trying to rebalance Britain and create a fairer and stronger economy had failed, leaving it one of the most unequal and divided countries in Europe. It urged:

"We need to adopt a strategy that allows London to sustain its global role while at the same time targeting some systematic firepower at raising the economic performance of regional Britain."[57]

And it pressed for a change to Treasury rules that made it harder to justify expenditure in less populous areas, thereby favouring London and the South East.

Of course, this is the levelling-up process to which the Conservative Prime Minister Boris Johnson is allegedly committed. So far it amounts to not much more than increased spending on roads, rail, schools, hospitals, and housing. There is little evidence of deep thinking on how the industrial and employment structure of regions outside London might be reshaped to reduce dependence on low-skilled and often impermanent jobs.

The Scots know what they would like to do differently, with all the powers of an independent state at their disposal. In most respects this represents a programme that a Welsh state would probably also want to follow, though the starting point would be further back in terms of existing economic strengths and institutional structures.

If the Sustainable Growth Commission's findings were implemented, the Scots would work up a model that used the three similarly sized economies of Denmark, Finland, and New Zealand. This, they note, is based on quality of governance, long term cross partisan strategy, a focus on innovation, competitiveness for international investment, exploitation of the country's resource endowment, export-orientation, immigration friendliness, maintenance of a highly skilled workforce and the use of the taxation system as a tool for economic development. For Wales, read Scotland.

The Welsh balance-sheet

Even so, it remains hard not to be brought back down to earth by the short, medium- or even long-term cost implications of opting for independence. Or, by the realisation that greater divergence rather than convergence with the rest of the UK economy may also be the result of maintaining the status quo, despite the Government's promised commitment to regional re-balancing.

Fortunately, reliable information is now available on the Welsh balance sheet through a report in early 2020 by the Wales Fiscal Analysis team at Cardiff University.[58] As a result the options can be considered more realistically than was the case previously. The UK Government's Office for Budget Responsibility has also this year produced its first Welsh taxes forecast. As such, we now have for the first-time detail on Welsh revenue and expenditure and the direction of travel. The stark truth: revenue raised in Wales is not set to show greater buoyancy but is set to decline further as a proportion of the total UK tax take.

However, before going further it is necessary to point out

that calculations in these reports are pre-Covid. All predictions regarding the economy of Wales, Britain, Europe, and the rest of the world are guesswork. We can only surmise what shape recovery will take or what industries and regions will suffer most or least, or what the tax take and revenue spending of the UK or Wales, and the consequent fiscal gaps or surpluses will be.

Nonetheless, in March 2020 it was possible for the Cardiff University report to state that at £13.5bn in 2018-19, the deficit between revenues raised in Wales and public spending in Wales was the second highest in the 12 UK planning regions after Northern Ireland. Public expenditure levels (outside certain areas such as infrastructure) are not, however, out of kilter with other regions. The Welsh deficit is primarily due to the lower tax revenues. In this respect Wales differs from Scotland where higher public spending accounts for the tax to spending deficit.

This lower Welsh tax take is mainly the consequence of lower wages. The UK income tax system is highly progressive, with by far the biggest share being contributed by higher income earners. Indeed, of the 440,000 additional rate taxpayers in the UK, 300,000 are in London and south-east England, compared with only 6,000 in Wales. Analysis by the Office of Budget Responsibility reveals that only 44 per cent of the Welsh population paid any income tax in 2016-17, compared with 47 per cent of the UK population (a bigger proportion of whom will have been paying higher rates).

With just under 5 per cent of the UK population Wales has only 1.4 per cent of additional rate taxpayers earning more than £150,000 a year. Low wage levels also exclude large numbers in Wales from paying National Insurance contributions. Welsh residents pay only 2.7 per cent of UK income tax revenues. If tax and National Insurance contributions in Wales matched the UK per person average, an additional £5.3bn would be raised.

Although high levels of Government spending in Wales

on social protection are maintaining living standards roughly equivalent to the rest of the UK, they are not contributing to the extent required to the rebuilding of the Welsh economic base. Infrastructure spending, essential to increasing the productivity and profitability of Welsh businesses, falls well short of spending in London and the South East where it is directed under current Treasury rules, because of the greater returns it will bring.

Thus, transport spending per head in Wales is less than half that in London, which has seen a succession of multi-billion pound rail projects over recent decades. This contrasts strongly with the struggle Wales has had to secure the funding for a potentially game-changing revamping of rail services into Cardiff. The current approach is to reward success in the south-east of England rather than remedy under-performance elsewhere, a point also made in the UK2070 report.

Paying our way

How to increase Wales's ability to pay its way, whether inside or outside GB, is the challenge. If GDP per person in Wales were to increase from its present level of 74 per cent of the UK average to 80 per cent by 2029-30, the deficit would, the authors of 'Wales' Fiscal Future' estimate, halve to around 9.4 per cent of GDP. Substantial growth in Welsh output, spurred by rapid productivity improvements, must occur for this to happen, but progress on this scale and beyond has proved elusive.

Militating against this, too, is the larger than average share of the Welsh population of people over 65 and therefore not economically active, and a smaller under-16 cohort entering the labour market. Emigration from rural areas and to universities in England never to return, in order to earn the higher wages – and pay higher taxes that their degree would facilitate – add to the problem.

Various reports have suggested that to catch up, Wales – irrespective of independence considerations – must adopt radical new policies and adopt a researched strategic approach. This must involve investing heavily in education, research and development, and infrastructure. Rebuilding would place a greater emphasis on local sourcing, the attraction of inward investment from growing sectors, and the maintenance and development of a stronger cadre of Welsh-owned and managed businesses. The attraction of entrepreneurial individuals and the retention or return of Welsh students whose skills are currently lost after graduation in English universities would also be required.

The hope that lies behind the case for status quo – union in a continuing United Kingdom with, or without Scotland – is that the policies outlined in the most recent iteration of Welsh Government economic policies, 'Prosperity for All, An Economic Action Plan', will work in combination with UK-sponsored 'levelling up'. Government funding will switch away from the South East, and road, rail and broadband infrastructure spending will be concentrated not just in the north of England and other English regions but will be made available to Wales, too.

In this scenario Britain will have other eggs than financial services in its basket and will be making more of the products on which it depends in basic fields, from foodstuffs to new areas in high technology and artificial intelligence. Many of the pioneering companies in these fields will decide to build in Wales (and similarly deprived English regions). Matching these developments Welsh schools will perform high up in the OECD Pisa league tables, and Welsh students will be trained in Welsh colleges and universities in the skills that successful economies of the future will depend on. Britain will have acquired once again the much more balanced economy that existed until several decades on after World War Two.

For all the good intentions of recent decades and the recent rhetoric of the UK Government, just how likely is this? The authors of 'Wales Fiscal Future' are sceptical. As they say:

"A key challenge for those who want Wales to remain a part of the UK revolves around the likelihood of Wales's current economic, fiscal and social problems being alleviated under current constitutional arrangements. Given the relative trends in the Welsh economy since 1999, there is room for doubt whether such a relative improvement in Wales's economic performance is possible, let alone likely."[59]

It would mean reversing more than 40 years of a largely *laissez-faire* approach to regional policy that has seen financial services become the dominant sector supporting the UK economy and allowing other sectors to grow more quickly in future. Moreover, it would be necessary to imagine a Cardiff Bay Government being able to exert considerable leverage on Westminster to secure the transformational expenditure and diversion of resources to Wales that will be needed.

A different sort of union

It is for this reason that independence has been advocated as a breakthrough option. 'Wales' Fiscal Future' makes clear that wide-ranging changes to both taxation and spending would be required from day one. Without fiscal transfers there would be a big bill to be paid in Wales for social security spending if current levels of service were to be maintained.

However, pension spending represents by far the largest part of UK government spending for Wales. The future financing of state pensions would need to be resolved before state separation. Currently the UK Government pays the pension of British citizens who have fulfilled their requirements to receive a state pension, regardless of whether they choose to retire within the UK. This would be the subject of negotiation between both governments. A continuation of the current practice could initially reduce Wales's deficit by £6billion a year or around 8 per cent of GDP, although this would gradually taper off as new Welsh pensioners start claiming from the Welsh state.

At the same time Wales would have to negotiate with the rest of the UK, in effect the Westminster Government, a settlement of the expenditure that would continue to be incurred to service Wales's proportion of inherited UK debt. Other costs, for example on border protection, for belonging to international institutions, paying for overseas healthcare or for culture and recreation services, including the BBC, are attributed proportionately to Wales at present and would either have to continue to be provided centrally and paid for, or replaced with separate Welsh-funded services, depending on the choices made.

The arrangements made with the rest of Britain for defence – whether a continuation of the present system of unified armed services or establishing a separate Welsh force – would also have to be determined and costed. Because many of these items of expenditure would have to be maintained, the savings from leaving the UK might not make much of a dent in the deficit. As noted earlier, an important exception is the cost of state old age pensions of £6bn, or 8 per cent of GDP, which is an obligation of the UK state.

Borrowing to replace the transfers now financing current account spending on benefits and other social protection would be an option. Because of the current world economic crisis, funds could indeed be obtained cheaply. Interest rates would still likely be higher than the UK is expected to pay, as lenders would factor in the default risks attached to lending to a new and potentially less creditworthy state.

In practice, a new Welsh Government would almost certainly

need to put in place fiscal consolidation measures – tax increases and/or spending cuts – with the aim of bringing down debt as a proportion of Gross Domestic Product. The authors of 'Wales' Fiscal Future' argue that closure of the deficit by 1.5 per cent a year would result in the debt to GDP peaking at 73 per cent in 2030-31. A 3 per cent a year improvement would see the ratio reach 44 per cent by 2026-27.

The shock to the system could be alleviated if Westminster could be persuaded to continue to make transfer payments tapering down over a period of say 20-25 years. The argument would be that an independent Wales capable of standing on its own feet would emerge, lifting a burden from the rest of Britain, and thus in its interests. Other regions of the UK would, however, have to be convinced and it could be a hard sell.

Whether or not this could be negotiated, what are the prospects of revenues raised internally, matching over time existing subventions from the centre? 'Wales' Fiscal Future' points to some areas where possible additional Welsh tax revenue might be raised, including from water and electricity supplies to other parts of the UK. However, given the competitive nature of the markets in which these utilities operate, it concludes the amounts would not be material. Desalination, in the case of water, and inter-connector supplies from France in the case of electricity would put a ceiling on the price Wales could demand.

A more promising approach might lie in a reformed tax system. An independent Wales would reconfigure the tax system to reflect the needs of the country. A modest but good recent example of the advantages of Wales determining its own tax system is the temporary changes made in the light of Covid-19 to the devolved Land Transaction Tax (LTT). In Wales the threshold was raised from £180,000 to £250,000 and second homes were not granted this relaxation of the rules. In England the equivalent Stamp Duty Land Tax (SDLT) threshold was increased from £125,000 to £500,000 and this applied to all homes including second homes. The resulting change in LTT in Wales applies to about 90 per cent of all transactions but will not stimulate further the second home market. In England it has been estimated that the average saving from the SDLT change will be £646 in north-east England, versus £15,000 in London. Once again, a tax policy, in this case for England only, formulated on a 'one size fits all' basis, is skewed heavily in favour of London and south-east England and in favour of purchasers of second homes.

As matters stand, the composition of the tax take in Wales differs in important ways from UK. Britain's income tax system is highly progressive. The highest earners make the biggest contribution, and this is even more marked in Wales where 46 per cent of the population pay no income tax, five percentage points higher than the equivalent proportion in UK. Higher rate tax is paid by 4.9 per cent of Welsh taxpayers, compared with 8.7 per cent in UK.

National Insurance revenues, another form of income tax levied on employees, are in line with the rest of the country but receipts from corporation tax are lower. Value Added Tax at 22.9 per cent of the total has recently become the principal revenue raiser in Wales, overtaking income tax, the biggest UK source of revenues accounting for 23.7 per cent of the total.

Higher taxes on high earners could, however, lead to their leakage across the border to England. Higher VAT rates would target spending not income, but would affect consumption and in practice add to the tax burden on poorer people not currently paying income tax. Higher tax rates on corporates could cause capital flight. Lower taxes, while potentially reducing revenue, could, however, lead to the attraction of companies (as Ireland has successfully demonstrated).

However, lower taxes might still require the acquiescence of the Treasury in England if retaliatory action was to be avoided.

Modest Welsh demands for powers to levy Air Passenger Duty to help Cardiff Airport have been firmly resisted on the grounds that it might harm Bristol, even though its passenger numbers are four times bigger, and it has big expansion plans.

Some critics see the projections in 'Wales' Fiscal Future' as too pessimistic. Swansea economist Dr John Ball argues that the corporation tax take attributed to Wales is too low. He also disputes the size of the expenditure allocations, which include, he argues, a share of funding for some schemes that benefit only England.[60]

While inevitable negotiations on tax variance with the rest of the UK would be tough, care would also be needed to ensure at least in the short to medium term that UK-facing public sector offices – the DVLA in Swansea, HMRC and Companies House in Cardiff and the Office for National Statistics in Newport for example – were not stripped away, as English regions might demand. Westminster might be persuaded to allow such agencies to operate outside English borders but only if the services they offered were competitive with rival bidders, and perhaps only if broadly similar systems and services applied in Wales.

Welsh taxes

These dilemmas have led to suggestions of other novel forms of taxation. Wales is a transit route for many of the goods travelling between Britain and Ireland yet provides the roads and other infrastructure for this service at no cost in tax to the user in the case of foreign vehicles. An independent Wales could replace fuel duty with a road pricing scheme. Electronically gathered, like the Dartford Crossing fee and the London congestion tax, this would harvest rent from trucks and other vehicles making regular usage of Welsh roads, including visitors to tourist destinations and vehicles travelling along the A55 and M4/A40 to and from

Ireland to England and the Continent. Such a levy would have to be set at a level that did not divert goods traffic to Liverpool and other ports and holidaymakers to other destinations.

A modest tourist tax could also be levied for use locally as happens in many US states and elsewhere. A pipeline tax on gas crossing from Milford Haven and a pylon tax on electricity leaving Wales are other possibilities, though neither of these would raise substantial revenue.

Plaid Cymru's leader, Adam Price, has suggested more purposeful use of existing Welsh-managed taxes might be implemented. One suggestion, a Land Value Tax would usefully target a non-mobile asset that, unlike individuals and their businesses, could not up sticks in protest. This could, he argues, generate £6bn on current values at a 3 per cent rate, making possible reductions or replacement of devolved taxes such as business rates and council taxes, and of income taxes (where the Welsh Government already has some limited variation powers).

A study into such a tax has indeed been prepared for the Welsh Government. Reporting early in 2020, it estimated that the total value of residential land in Wales was £113.4billion, and the total value of land underlying properties which currently pay non-domestic rates was £27.6billion. A uniform national LVT rate of 1.41 per cent on residential land would be sufficient to raise the same revenues as are currently raised by council tax. A uniform national LVT rate of 3.9 per cent charged on the properties that currently pay non-domestic rates would be sufficient to replace that tax. Higher or lower rates, adjusted to local circumstances, could bring in extra resources or reduce the burden where deemed appropriate.

A UK common market

Other issues facing the Scots, and extensively rehearsed during the Scottish referendum campaign in 2014, would be replicated in any new referendum north of the border, and in Wales, which in any case is unlikely to progress towards independence or even a ballot before the Scots. Arguments over currency, trade barriers, monetary policy, and historic debt featured strongly then and would do so again if the SNP Government in Edinburgh were to win a second referendum during the next decade.

In a post-Brexit world the degree of integration of the two countries into the UK economy – the most important export market being England – suggests both (and Wales especially) would find it impossible not to be part of a UK Single Market, rather than standing alone. (Whether or not it would be a Britain and Northern Ireland market will depend on the constitutional and/or trading status of Northern Ireland remaining the same as relations between the UK and the EU bed down post-Brexit.)

Within such a market, an independent Wales would not be able to enter separate trade deals with other blocs or nations, and would anyway lack the capacity to do so, possibly for many years. It would instead have to adopt arrangements negotiated for the whole market. Wales would be expected to demand representation within negotiating parties but might in practice be in no stronger a position to influence outcomes than it is now.

It is possible to consider the notion of Wales leaving the rest of the UK common trading area and joining the European Union (as the current Scottish Government wishes to do) at some point in the future. However, this could only occur many decades ahead, after Wales had engineered a transformation in its trading profile, replacing its closely interwoven trade links with England with similar close links with Benelux, Germany, France, and other EU countries.

Wales has a slightly bigger share of exports heading for the

EU than the UK generally, but probably a similar import profile. However, the bulk of these exports are concentrated in a few products and sectors, notably aircraft wings and other aviation components, vehicle engines and refined oil products. Most Welsh businesses are not engaged in exporting. It would be unrealistic, therefore, to suggest that Wales, as Scotland envisages, might seek entry to the EU post-independence, if England chose not to do so.

An export growth strategy designed to increase the value of exports, and diversify sources of export income, as the Irish have done, is one of the main recommendations in the Scottish report and would be even more necessary in the case of Wales – which does not have the huge export-orientated whisky sector or even a declining oil asset as a foundation stone of its overseas sales – to reduce dependence on the English market.

There is a parallel here with Ireland, which, as its economy stood at the time, could only follow the lead of the UK when the decision to join the EU was taken by the Conservative government in Britain in 1974. Such was Ireland's dependence on the UK at that stage it would have been impossible for it to join separately or stay outside once Britain had decided to enter. Over the past 40 years this situation has changed considerably. Ireland has built up an enviable export trade with the EU and the rest of the world in food, pharmaceuticals, industrial equipment, computers, mineral ores, and other products, and can regard Britain's departure from the bloc with equanimity and comfortably remain a member independently.

The long drawn-out negotiations over the land border between the Irish Republic and Northern Ireland, resulting in a very unclear arrangement which may not long survive implementation, offer a further caution. The arrangements for trade between Wales in the EU and England outside would be equally if not more difficult to formalise.

Again, links with England make it more difficult to argue the case for a separate Welsh currency. Though countries as small or even smaller than Wales have proved capable of managing a currency of their own, a Welsh currency would impose transaction costs on businesses that would make Welsh operations less competitive than those on the other side of the border with England. However, there are advantages in having a separate currency, not least the ability to revalue as appropriate to reflect changes in competitiveness, but these longer-term benefits would have to be forsaken if immediate damage to Welsh firms was to be avoided.

There are similarities here, too, with Ireland. Before both countries entered the European Communities (as it then was), Ireland was part of the sterling area with the same coins and notes but bearing Irish symbols.

On Irish entry into the Exchange Rate Mechanism in 1979, the Irish punt decoupled from the £ sterling and a separate central bank was created. This allowed the punt to move up and down against sterling, sometimes being more valuable and sometimes less, reflecting the month-by-month competitiveness of the Irish economy *vis à vis* the UK. The punt ceased to exist when Ireland joined the euro.

These limitations expose a further problem. If a post-independence Wales were to share a common currency with the remainder of the UK it would have to negotiate the right to share in decisions on monetary and interest rate policy. Leverage, however, would rest very heavily with rest of the UK.

So, while independence can be promoted as a way out of Wales's chronic weaknesses economically and socially, there are limitations on the extent of that status. Links with England, in what would remain a union to a lesser or greater extent, would need to be factored in.

A middle way

In the immediate future a two-stage process might be the way ahead. Rebuilding the economy has been a Sisyphean task for the past four generations. It must continue to be a priority of the Welsh Government which should insist it stands at the heart of the UK Government agenda.

Now that recovery from the Covid-19 pandemic is beginning and other issues can be brought forward, UK Government must be held to its promises to level up the UK economy in a meaningful way. Even more importantly, the current Welsh Government, and its successor in 2021, needs to ensure that its voice is heard as loudly as that of the Midlands and North of England, now under the leadership of increasingly vocal mayors.

Against Treasury restrictions, the Welsh Government must endeavour to increase its capacity to borrow for capital spending. It must also have more leeway to shape Welsh business to meet domestic needs without any impact on the Treasury block grant Wales receives. These measures will add to the Welsh deficit and to Government debt. However, they will have the effect of reversing rather than ameliorating current economic weaknesses, as the present funding arrangements seek to do. In other words, an ambitious investment programme to 'pump prime' the Welsh economy is required: an approach which was abandoned by UK governments when the UK joined the EU.

The key demand must be that additional finance is deployed through borrowing and, more importantly, through the proposed UK Shared Prosperity Fund. This will need to go beyond the EU funding that is being lost, so that Wales and other regions can protect against climate change and develop the industries needed for this purpose. Wales will want to improve its transport and technological infrastructure, strengthen its local economies, and participate fully in modern business sectors.

Wales must become less dependent on FDI, and branch

factories. The needs of its population dictate the necessity of more technologically-advanced businesses, more locally-owned businesses, more headquarters businesses, better education for work in business, and more effectively-trained managers. It wants to be making greater use of its natural resources to develop a strong food and agriculture sector, its creative industries, its financial and professional services, its biosciences, tourism, and leisure activities. More research into the business needs of the Welsh economy is a priority.

In short, Wales needs an economy that is much more like Denmark or Ireland to make independence seem a realistic prospect for the people of Wales. The challenge is to demonstrate the kind of economy and society that Wales would seek to create and ensure it is one that Welsh people would be comfortable to choose. A significant strengthening of the economy in the short and medium term will improve the lot of Welsh people and, further ahead, put Wales in a position where an independence option can be put forward that would seem less of a risky leap of faith.

Sceptics will still have a field day and in fairness the record to date is not encouraging. However, a simple question can be posed. If Ireland had not decided 100 years ago to break with Britain, would it now be among the richest parts of these Isles, up there with London and the South East? Or would it be poor old Ireland, down there with Wales as one of the weakest of the 12 UK economic planning regions?

Recommendations

1. The role of the Welsh civil service should be re-examined to separate economic policymaking and implementation.
2. A new agency or agencies should be established to promote

small business growth, medium size business development, inward investment, productivity, and export activity.

3. A new inward investment focus is needed on businesses capable of offering high quality jobs, even if initially in small numbers, in technology, health and sophisticated consumer-facing products. Potential investors in new technology nations need to be cultivated and contact deepened with alumni of Welsh universities overseas.

4. The export propensity of Welsh firms needs to be encouraged and stimulated to increase revenues and help increase the productivity and scale of Welsh business. Wales should search for businesses that might be relocated back in Britain for strategic security, environmental or other reasons.

5. The role of the Welsh Development Bank should be expanded to ensure that state support for key sectors can take the form of direct Welsh Government stakes.

6. Greater involvement with the venture capital industry should be sought and a Welsh venture capital trust investing in Welsh start-ups established.

7. The foundation economy should be put at the centre of policymaking and incentives and penalties to secure greater public sector purchasing put in place. A wholesaler type body should be created to aggregate private sector provision and support tendering, together with a facility through which companies could make their offering more widely known.

8. In the aftermath of the Covid-19 crisis a window for a much greater emphasis on local production and procurement will open and this must be seized. Support should be given to businesses seeking to re-shore products currently made elsewhere, and further efforts made to ensure Welsh food producers contribute a bigger share of the nation's food purchases.

9. An incoming Government should review the entire Welsh higher education sector to ensure its priority is meeting the needs of the Welsh economy and society. It should set in motion measures to encourage more Welsh students to stay in Wales for their degrees and their subsequent careers, and that those going elsewhere are encouraged to return.

10. Policymakers need to be equipped with better business intelligence on the needs of the Welsh economy. Welsh Government and business should back the creation of a new university centre for the study of Welsh business and business needs.

CHAPTER 6

Wales and Europe

O UR DISCUSSION OF WALES'S future relationship with the European Union must be set in the context of the grave and constantly shifting crisis facing humanity and the planet which we inhabit. This crisis is multi-faceted.

Underlying everything is the issue of the sustainability of the natural world of which humanity is one part, and upon which it is entirely dependent for its well-being. Hugely damaging climate change resulting from greenhouse gas emissions is at last receiving the attention that it deserves after decades of unforgiveable neglect. Equally significant however is the collapse of biodiversity arising from the increasing encroachment of humanity on the natural world in pursuit of the constant growth that underpins our present way of life.

This calls into question the sustainability of an economic system beset also by a whole series of other challenges ranging from technological change to the grotesque gap between rich and poor both within and between countries and regions.

The Covid-19 pandemic threatens to throw the economy into a state of chaotic breakdown whose outcome it is impossible to predict but is certain to be far-reaching.

It is easier to speculate than to pontificate about the effects of this multiple crisis, the elements of which are deeply interrelated. For example, it may force a greater degree of localisation as the vulnerability of long-distance supply-chains and the massive environmental impact of haulage and incessant mobility are exposed. Certain aspects of globalisation may be called into question. On the other hand, the dynamic growth of electronic communication will strengthen globalisation and may have the effect of reducing the significance of locality as such.

What must be beyond speculation is that we cannot hope to respond constructively to the current crisis without unprecedented international co-operation and a vision of humanity as one global family. Isolationism and reactionary nationalism may be a tempting response to the situation in which we find ourselves but is certain to be utterly counter-productive. More than ever we need a far more effective global architecture of governance to address the climate change, migration and health issues that face the world, empowered to cope with crises as they arise and to plan for a sustainable future. In the wake of the pandemic the World Health Organisation is currently one very special case in point.

We see it as an error of tragic proportions that, at this moment, Britain has left the European Union, a unique experiment in transnational governance and sovereignty-sharing whose contribution to global co-operation has been enormous. The proposals of the present UK Government for the terms of that departure, with Europe and the world desperately seeking to cope with the effects of pandemic, threaten to turn tragedy into catastrophe.

In the following chapter we discuss the possibility of an independent Wales, separately from England, becoming either a member-state of the EU, or, failing that, establishing a close relationship through membership of Efta and the EEA.

In this chapter we set out some ideas about how Wales might in the meanwhile start the process of building a new relationship with Europe.

Plaid Cymru and Europe

The ideal of building a new Wales as a fully-fledged European nation has informed Plaid Cymru's thinking since its establishment. In his lecture to Plaid Cymru's very first conference in 1926, Saunders Lewis, warned against the kind of extreme, unbridled nationalism that had disfigured Europe over the centuries, and identified a united Europe, with Wales a participant in its own right, as a key aim.

The fundamental purpose of the European Community which emerged after the Second World War was to promote peace and reconciliation. The European Coal and Steel Community which was its starting point was about controlling 'the engines of war'. The 1972 Paris Declaration of the EEC Heads of State and Governments, issued on the eve of the first enlargement comprising Denmark, Ireland and the UK, made it clear that this new unique experiment in sovereignty-sharing and transnational governance was about infinitely more than developing a 'common market'.

That declaration established the objective of economic and monetary union but also emphasised non-material values. It called for an action plan to protect the natural environment and for a regional development fund to "correct the structural and regional imbalances in the Community". The need for co-operation with the so-called 'Third World' was also highlighted.

It is hardly surprising therefore that Saunders Lewis was taken aback by Plaid Cymru's decision to oppose British membership in the confirmatory referendum in 1975, after Britain had joined the European Community in 1973. This was partly on the grounds that Wales would have no representation within the Community's institutions. Another reason given was that, despite the Paris Agreement's commitment to an active regional policy, the reality of an unfettered common market would favour prosperous regions and be detrimental to an outlying, underdeveloped economy such as Wales.

However, by the late 1980s Plaid's position had changed fundamentally. A number of factors contributed to this shift.

As the European Community succeeded and grew, Plaid members became increasingly aware that it offered an alternative reference point for Wales to England and London. At the same time the EU's own recognition of the rich internal diversity of Europe and the role of the sub-state nations, regions and localities was becoming more explicit and active. One example of this, part of the wider involvement in education and culture seen as essential to the development of Europe, was the support for lesser-used languages which provided opportunities for collaboration and cultural exchange, in which many Plaid members participated. The European Parliament played a key role in initiating this. At the same time the European Commission was giving practical effect to its commitment to economic and social cohesion, providing substantial financial support for regenerating the economies of disadvantaged regions such as Wales. Meanwhile, and despite its imperfections, the Common Agricultural Policy benefited Welsh farmers and rural communities.

Thus, Plaid Cymru actively supported the ratification of the Maastricht Treaty which created the European Union, strengthened the European structural funds, and recognised the importance of the sub-state level by establishing the Committee of the Regions, on which Wales was represented.

The introduction of democratic devolved government for Wales in 1999 coincided with greatly expanded resources from the European structural funds coming to Wales: over £4bn during the period 2000-2020. The way in which these and other funding streams were deployed is discussed below.

Brexit and devolution

The narrow majority in Wales in favour of leaving the European Union in the 2016 referendum came as a bitter blow to Plaid Cymru. The party's initial response was to accept the result but to press for Britain to remain within the European Customs Union and Single Market. This policy was set out in a joint document with the Welsh Government, 'Securing Wales's Future: transition from the EU to a new relationship with Europe'. Despite the SNP's renewed call for a referendum on Scottish independence following Scotland's unequivocal support for remaining in the EU, the Scottish Government adopted a similar position with regard to the UK's withdrawal proposals. However, as it became clear that the UK Government was bent not only on leaving the Customs Union and Single Market, but also distancing itself from EU policies and programmes across the board, Plaid Cymru, along with the SNP, supported the demands for a second referendum with a view to remaining in the EU.

Brexit soon led to a major conflict between the UK Government and those of Wales, Scotland and Northern Ireland by exposing the vulnerabilities of devolved government against a UK parliamentary majority. Working together, the Welsh and Scottish Governments withheld approval of the 2018 EU Withdrawal Bill. The Welsh Government, having gained certain concessions, withdrew its opposition but the Scottish Government held firm.

In 2020, the Welsh Government, having noted that the Withdrawal Agreement left wide open the position on a range of EU policies and programmes which directly influenced Wales, yet again refused assent, along with the Scottish Government. Nevertheless, the UK Government carried on regardless.

As well as the UK Government's position on leaving the Customs Union and Single Market, the definition of the devolved administrations' powers was a bone of contention. The

109

Sewell Convention, which stated that the UK Parliament would not normally legislate on devolved matters without the consent of the devolved legislatures, lacked legal force. This became a live issue as the EU legislative framework in devolved fields such as agriculture, social well-being and the environment was scheduled to come to an end with Brexit. The UK Government's interpretation was that the 'repatriated powers' should become the responsibility of the UK Government, while the devolved administrations saw this as an attempt to seize powers which constitutionally belonged to them. The 2017 Wales Act, which in principle replaced the conferred powers model of devolution with a reserved powers model, was seen as failing to address this issue.

A further significant question is how, following Brexit, the UK's proposed substitute for the European Structural and Investment Funds (the 'Shared Prosperity Fund'), will be administered. At present the European Funds are administered jointly by the EU Commission and the nominated Managing Authorities, which in the case of Wales, Scotland and Northern Ireland, are their devolved governments. The Welsh Government has made clear that it should have responsibility for the delivery of the Shared Prosperity Fund. However, despite Brexit taking place at the end of January 2020, that matter has been left unresolved.

EU Funding for Wales: a lost opportunity

The establishment of the National Assembly coincided with the EU's recognition of 'West Wales and the Valleys' as a 'less-developed region', with a per-head GDP of less than 75 per cent of the EU average. Cornwall and the Isles of Scilly was the only other of 40 UK sub-regions to be thus designated, an indication of the grave weakness of the Welsh economy at that time. This particular designation was advantageous not only in terms of the total sums available but because 'less developed regions' were allowed greater flexibility in their use of those funds than those receiving European support through other designations.

Despite a strong challenge from Plaid, Labour was able to form the first democratic devolved government of Wales in 1999 and subsequently consolidate its position by forming a coalition with the Liberal Democrats. Thus, Labour remained in power as significant streams of European funding became available for Wales.

The new Government had to work within certain constraints. It soon emerged that it was far from certain that the EU funds would be truly additional to the block grant which Westminster provided for the delivery of devolved functions (the 'Welsh block'). Funding to Wales under previous designations such as Objective 5b had, it now became clear, always led to the reduction of an equivalent sum from the Welsh block. In 2000, following a political crisis in the National Assembly in which Alun Michael resigned as First Secretary, the UK Chancellor Gordon Brown provided a guarantee of additionality. Despite this, the Welsh Assembly Government, as it then chose to call itself, found itself obliged to match European funds with monies from its own budget rather than the UK Government acting in the spirit of EU regional policy and providing that 'match funding'. Moreover, the National Assembly lacked legislative, taxation, and borrowing powers and other levers for economic renewal.

It is nevertheless the case that the EU pumped significant extra sums into Wales which provided a great opportunity for economic renewal. However, what the Welsh Government lacked was a coherent vision for the growth of Wales as a European nation. Strategy is the daughter of vision, and its absence was seen in the way European funds were spent over the years on a multiplicity of projects. Many were worthwhile in themselves, but they lacked the overall strategic planning that could have had a transformational systemic effect.

One aspect of this was a failure to identify and target key strategic areas and to ensure synergy across policy fields to achieve specific objectives. This was accompanied by a failure to link developments in Wales with key European policy priorities. The result was that Wales failed to be at the vanguard of forward-looking policy innovation.

Another consequence was the inability to make strategic use of the European Regional Development and Social Funds to take proper advantage of other funding streams such as Erasmus, Horizon and Creative Europe which were hugely significant for Welsh higher and further education.

These failings were identified in the 2016 report to Welsh Government by the 'Wales EU Funding Ambassadors' who also stated:

> "We have observed that the engagement of Wales with the EU, outside the areas of the Structural Funds and Common Agricultural Policy, does not have the depth, strategic content and coherence that one would expect through comparison with other similar regions."[61]

It is nevertheless only fair to acknowledge that where synergies were actually secured there have been some notable success stories.

The European Union's direction of travel

At the same time as Britain was leaving the EU, the remaining 27 states were redoubling their efforts strategically to address the range of challenges and opportunities that it confronts in an age of critical change.

The coming few years will see a succession of EU summits

progressively building up the Union's collective capacity to attack the economic, social, health and healthcare consequences of the Covid-19 pandemic. This process will reflect the internal political and public debates within member states on both the short-term and long-term impacts of this global crisis. It will shape and determine the scale and ambition of the gearing up of EU strategy and financing for the remainder of this decade. The aim will be to reinforce the thrust of the EU's strategic position defined prior to the outbreak of the pandemic.

Application of the principle of economic and social cohesion was already established as a centrepiece of the EU strategy. It was set when President Delors made it a central strategic commitment in the 1980s, as the necessary counterweight to the operation of the internal market. This commitment to shared solidarity will now have to be scaled up substantially with an EU recovery package, mobilising all the EU's financial instruments to address the damage inflicted by the pandemic.

The institutions of the EU will face difficult choices in designing this package. They will have to reach agreement on the terms that will govern the solidarity measures initiated. In so doing there they will have to find a way of securing a new political consensus across the member states. It will involve the European Council adopting the EU's Multiannual Financial Framework (MFF) for the period until 2028.

In July 2020, a five-day European Council agreed a €750 billion pandemic recovery package, of which an unprecedented €390 billion was in grants, not repayable loans. The heads of government also agreed a seven-year budget of more than €1 trillion. To pay for the collective borrowing programme, unprecedented in itself, the summit also agreed – in principle – to new common taxes. These include levies on plastics and polluting imports and a digital tax.

Taken together, the package is likely to prove a radical step towards creating an EU fiscal policy. It was the first significant move towards an eventual system of EU economic governance since the era of Jacques Delors as Commission President in the 1990s. It reflected both the revival of the Franco–German alliance and the political impact of Brexit, in this case the absence from the negotiating table of a sceptical UK government.[62]

This cohesive response of the EU is likely to prove highly significant across the continent as all member states struggle to deal with the repercussions of the pandemic. The EU itself will have to deal with competitive advantages or disadvantages which will result from state interventions (that is, state aids), affecting the operation of the 'level playing field' principles underpinning the integrity of the Internal Market, to which the EU is firmly attached.

The damage inflicted on European and international supply chains will be a critical preoccupation, as in some cases they may be permanently affected. At the same time continuing concern about a further outbreak of the pandemic will emphasise the need to prioritise investment in health and healthcare systems, education, research and innovation.

The accelerating impact of job losses and firm closures will fuel public concern especially when evidence emerges of unemployment figures exploding across the age groups, exacerbating the present sharp divide between the haves and the have nots.

The present economic and social policy framework within member states and at EU level is likely be severely challenged. In the UK, this framework has already been undermined through a period of continual cuts in public services and growing social inequalities. This framework will be increasingly seen as 'unfit for purpose' in the present turbulent and unpredictable environment. There will be demands for imaginative new policies to meet the challenges we all must face.

Now is not the time to reduce the role of the state. Rather there will be a need for more systemic interventions by the public sector in economic and social life.

Brexit and the terms of departure

At the end of 2020 a Trade and Cooperation Agreement was reached between the European Union and the UK Government. Although no substitute for the benefits the UK already had from being inside the EU Single Market and Customs Union, the Agreement softened the UK's borders with the EU, removing tariffs on most manufacturing and agricultural products.

Although this deal was preferable to leaving without an agreement, it came nowhere near to meeting the demands made by the Welsh Government in its January 2020 document 'The Future UK/EU relationship: Negotiating Priorities for Wales'.[63] Among those priorities were:

- Placing the fullest possible access to EU markets ahead of the UK's prioritisation of the UK's freedom to diverge from EU regulation.
- Publication by the UK Government of an assessment of the economic impact of non-tariff and, possibly, tariff barriers to exports, including on Wales.
- Dynamic alignment with EU regulations rather than establishing a parallel regulatory regime for the UK.
- Continued participation in EU programmes: Erasmus+, Horizon Europe, the Ireland Wales programme and Creative Europe.

When the UK Government published its negotiating mandate in February there was little indication that any attention had been paid to the Welsh or any other devolved government's representations. Counsel General and Brexit Minister Jeremy

Miles expressed his intense frustration with the UK Government's attitude, specifically in relation to the European programmes, thus:

> "We have...repeatedly made the case for the UK to negotiate continued participation in a number of successor EU programmes. Here the UK Government has sought to make decisions on what they see as in the best interests of England. We have repeatedly argued the case for the UK Government to negotiate the option for Wales to continue to participate in EU programmes even if the UK Government does not do so for England. They have chosen not to do so and the mandate only includes somewhat begrudging references to participating in a narrow range of programmes."[64]

What all this signifies is not only the havoc that the UK Government's policy on Brexit is certain to wreak on the Welsh economy, but its deeply unsatisfactory approach to inter-governmental relations, and, at a deeper level, current constitutional arrangements. The UK Government is both willing and able to ride rough-shod over the interests of Wales and Scotland in relation to a range of critically important policy areas. It is further evidence of the need for the kind of fundamental changes that we advocate in this report.

The Trade and Co-operation Agreement reached between the UK and the EU at the end of 2020 did not settle the Brexit process. Instead, it was only the beginning of what will be constant negotiations over the future relationship between the UK and the EU that are likely to become permanent. These will be overseen by a new UK/EU bureaucracy, a Joint Partnership Council serviced by at least 30 committees and working groups. Among the unknown factors that will influence future developments are whether:

- The new arrangements will lead to further softening of

the UK/EU border, for example with the trade agreement being extended to financial services.

- The Welsh and Scottish Governments are able to pursue bilateral links with the EU, for example by joining the Erasmus scheme on their own account.

We need to remind ourselves how grievous is the threat to Wales if the UK Government continues to pursue its present intentions. The UK Government's stated intention to diverge from European human rights, social and environmental standards may well be inimical to Wales. As a third country, with no seat at the EU decision-making table, the UK will need to pay for access to European programmes such as Horizon and Erasmus. We in Wales must vigorously argue the case in favour of doing so.

Wales has been a major beneficiary of European funding streams for research and innovation, including the Horizon programme. Wales receives only 2 per cent of UK research funding compared with England's 89 per cent and Scotland's 7 per cent. In stark contrast, in 2014-20 ERDF funding for research and innovation allocated 55 per cent (81m euros) to England; 26 per cent (28m euros) to Wales; and 11 per cent (15m euros) to Scotland.[65]

The UK Government's proposal to replace European regional development funds with a 'Shared Prosperity Fund' remains undeveloped and leaves many questions unanswered, including:

- What will be the sums available?
- What will be the length of the funding period?
- How will the funds be administered, given that this is a devolved policy function?

If common sense prevails and the UK remains part of the Horizon and Erasmus programmes (there is a stated intention to leave Creative Europe), future Welsh Governments will need to be ingenious in seeking opportunities for linking whatever European resources remain accessible to Wales's developmental priorities.

Whatever the nature of the so-called new partnership between the UK and EU, Wales needs to be keenly aware of developments in the EU where much of the agenda for future economic, social and environmental development will be set. The UK's departure from the EU should make us all the more determined to seek a new, autonomous, relationship between Wales and the EU.

A new relationship with the European Union

At this point it is worth recalling the way in which the Welsh engagement with the EU has grown over the last three decades.[66] During the 1980s awareness grew of the significance of the European dimension, particularly in relation to the sub-state level.

The case was made for Wales to become involved in what has been described as 'para-diplomacy'. In 1992 a formal Welsh presence in Brussels was established through the Wales European Centre, sponsored by the Welsh Development Agency and Welsh Local Government Association but with the involvement also, among others, of the Training and Enterprise Councils, Welsh universities and the Wales Council for Voluntary Action. This partnership approach to lobbying on Wales's behalf at Brussels bore dividends – not least in the granting of Objective 1 funding status for West Wales and the Valleys.

After the advent of devolved government in 1999 the model changed. Welsh Government took overall responsibility and is now co-located in Brussels at Wales House with Wales Higher Education and the National Assembly (now the Senedd/Welsh Parliament). The Welsh Local Government Association ceased its involvement in 2018.

Wales also enjoys full accreditation as part of the UK's Permanent Representation (UKRep) to the EU. Welsh Ministers participate in the UK Government's delegations at negotiations in the Council of Ministers on devolved policy areas. Welsh officials are also involved in preparatory meetings.

The key functions of the Welsh Government's presence in Brussels, as more generally abroad, are: (i) intelligence gathering; (ii) policy influence; (iii) profile raising; and (iv) partnership building.

European networks

One important means of fulfilling these functions is participation in European networks, which provide structures for exchanging information, policy development and collaborative working. Following Britain's departure from the EU, these networks will become even more significant as a means of intelligence gathering and wielding Welsh influence.

Welsh Government participates in a number of pan-European networks including:

- The Conference of Peripheral and Maritime Regions, which works across a range of policy areas.
- The Vanguard Initiative for innovation and smart specialisation in industry.
- Associate membership of the Four Motors of Europe, which aims to promote the knowledge economy at the regional level.

Other Welsh organisations are also involved in pan-European activity, for example:

- The Senedd/Welsh Parliament participates in the Conference of European Regional Legislative Assemblies.
- The Welsh Local Government Association is a member of the Council of European Municipalities and Regions.
- Cardiff is a member of EUROCITIES.

Bilateral relationships

The Brussels Office assists the Welsh Government in supporting formal and informal alliances with other small nations and regions across Europe, including:

- Brittany.
- Euskadi, the Basque Country.
- Galicia.
- Nord Holland.
- Flanders.

The Memorandum of Understanding with Brittany provides examples of how these relationships work in practice. Areas of activity are:

- Strengthening economic co-operation.
- Collaboration in education and training, including youth exchanges.
- Exchanges between cultural networks.
- Sharing best practice in language planning.
- Sharing experience in fields such as cybersecurity, sustainable development, renewable energy, tourism, and agri-foods.

Welsh Government's International Strategy

In 2020 the Welsh Government published its 'International Strategy', a document setting out its proposals for developing Wales's role in the world, including particularly the EU. It identified three core ambitions:

- Raising Wales's profile internationally, and presenting Wales as a country of creativity, innovation and experiment.
- Growing the economy, emphasising inward investment and embracing new technology.

- Global responsibility and sustainability, referencing the Well-being of Future Generations Act.

Welsh Government sees strengthening links with the EU as central to its strategy. Over the next five years it commits to increase "… our presence in EU member states and work to ensure that the European Union remains our strongest partner with whom we share many values and policy ambitions, and with whom we wish to continue to trade as efficiently as possible in the future". This will involve:

- Developing a strong Welsh Government office in Brussels as part of a wider Wales House with other partners.
- Continuing to collaborate with other partners including other regional offices and networks.
- Understanding and seeking to influence the effect of the EU on Wales.
- Influencing the UK Government and its agencies and other devolved governments to ensure that Welsh needs are considered.

More specifically, the intention is to 'build on existing Memoranda of Understanding, by working with governments in our key partner countries and regions to develop relationships whereby Wales can benefit economically, culturally and socially'.

Deepening Wales's relationship with the EU

A Plaid Cymru government should build upon these proposals and ensure that they are implemented effectively. It should however go further. A Plaid Welsh Government should explore the possibility of establishing a special relationship between Wales and the EU, in the short term as a sub-state nation. The possibility of continuing to participate in Erasmus and Horizon should be a priority.

Another possibility would be for the Welsh Government to examine the scope for reaching agreement with the European Commission to enable certain specified products from Wales to have unfettered access to the Single Market. Welsh Government could establish an inspectorate to certify that products of companies participating in the scheme complied fully with EU regulations. Membership of the scheme would be voluntary but rigorously applied, with penalties for any failure to meet the specified standards. A further possibility would be to establish a port which would export only goods in this category and where entry to the EU would be allowed without formalities.[67]

In exploring and seeking a form of alternative status in relation to the EU, Wales should cultivate a closer collaborative relationship with Ireland. Collaboration already exists, for example with the recent re-opening of the Irish consulate in Cardiff, and the Ireland Wales Programme (see below). Despite the loss of European Interreg funding, that economic collaboration should be extended beyond the existing areas.

The Welsh-Irish relationship should go well beyond collaboration on specific economic and cultural projects. There is a profound affinity between Wales and Ireland as Celtic nations historically absorbed through force of arms within the British state but which in the course of the 20th century have reasserted their identities as political nations – Ireland as an independent republic, and Wales as a devolved nation with aspirations to independence. For us in Wales, Ireland serves as a model of a successful small nation, a significant player within the EU and on the world stage.

We therefore recommend that the Welsh Government should establish a particular, special relationship with Ireland, among other things as a friend at the European court and an advocate on our behalf as we redefine and build our new role in relation to the EU.

Developing that role has implications for the machinery of government in Wales. In evidence presented to the External Affairs Committee of the National Assembly, Hywel Ceri Jones, an EU Funding Ambassador, recommended that the Welsh Government should establish a strong central strategic unit to deal with international affairs. It would need to have:

"... the intersectoral capacity, combined with experience and expertise on EU relations and the range of EU policies and programmes, to drive an... effective plan of action for Wales'.[68]

Despite the inevitable loss of the EU structural funds and the threat to other EU funding streams, we believe that such an entity within Welsh Government, working closely with Wales House in Brussels, is necessary for Wales to develop its relationship with the EU.

In Wales as in Brussels, the Welsh Government must see itself as part of a partnership, working with universities, local government, the trade unions and business. This kind of active partnership has been a key component in Ireland's economic success over the decades. It would also encourage all levels of Welsh society to become actively involved in European affairs

Another aspect of collaboration would be for the Welsh Government, with the involvement of MSs and Welsh MPs, to establish mechanisms to maintain a close dialogue, including exchanges of information and experience, with EU institutions, in particular the European Parliament, the Committee of the Regions and the Economic and Social Committee.

Growing European partnerships

Membership of the EU and funding from the various sources has enabled Wales to develop partnerships with other European nations and regions. Part of our response to Brexit must be to persist in nurturing these partnerships. This is an important way in which Wales can continue to be involved in the European enterprise, whatever happens in England. There can also be serious practical outcomes despite the non-availability of significant funding streams.

Ireland, a member state, and Euskadi (the Basque Country), a sub-state nation, provide two examples. Both of these nations have succeeded in transforming their economies in a way that has so far eluded Wales. Both provide role models from which Wales can learn.

Ireland

Ireland famously has succeeded in harnessing its status as a member state to access funding streams that have allowed it to progress from being one of the most economically challenged of western European economies to becoming one of the most advanced. Crucial to its success was its strategic approach to development, expressed as the 'four claws of the Celtic Tiger':

- Strong inward investment.
- Partnership agreements and pacts between government and the employers and trade unions.
- Transformation of the quality of education and training.
- Combining domestic and EU funding in an explicitly concerted drive of policy development.'[69]

Between 2014 and 2020, 80 million euros were provided for the Ireland Wales programme under Interreg, part of the EU's Territorial Co-operation Programme. This entailed investment in research and innovation, business engagement, and workforce development. The regions included in the programme are mainly coastal, extending from Meath to Kerry in Ireland, and from Wrexham as far as Swansea in Wales. The wide range of projects underway include:

- Ports Past and Present, which explores the cultures of Dublin, Rosslare, Holyhead, Fishguard and Pembroke Dock with a view to raising public awareness, enhancing visitor awareness and increasing capacity to utilise the natural and cultural heritage to drive economic growth.
- BRAINWAVES, which develops technology to manage slurry and dirty water and enhance the competitiveness of the beef and dairy industry.
- Selkie, which encourages the growth of ocean-base renewable energy industries.
- Catalyst, which works with 60 companies on innovation in life sciences and the food and drink industry.
- More than a Club, to assist local football clubs to develop social enterprises.
- Echoes, ccat, STREAM and Ecostructure which promote adaptation to climate change.
- Celtic Routes, which develop cultural tourism.

Euskadi (the Basque Country)

Euskadi and Wales have much in common, in terms of size and topography, a commitment to restore their lesser-used national languages, and an economic history involving decline of traditional industries. What has been different is Euskadi's success, since the achievement of self-government as an autonomous community in 1978, in revitalising its economy on a new basis. Wales has a great deal to learn from the Basque example and the Wales-Basque partnership provides an important opportunity to do so.

Euskadi has pioneered in the field of comprehensive language planning, achieving remarkable success at expanding Basque-medium education, making significant gains in inter-generational language transmission, and promoting widespread usage of the language. These achievements provide a model from which we can learn as we embark on the project of having a million Welsh-speakers by 2050.

A recent event organised by Orkestra, the Basque Institute of Competitiveness, and Cardiff University, including representatives from the Welsh Government, provides one illustration of the continuing potential for European partnership.[70] The event aimed to:

- Explore strategies for smart specialisation based on the public, private and university sectors in both countries.
- Establish strategic research and innovation partnerships to accelerate the development of industry, particularly SMEs.

Basque success sprang from an enthusiastic sense of identity and national purpose, strong government which has been closely involved in economic transformation, together with strategic consistency and stability over four decades.

Following a detailed exploration of the potential for partnership working, bilateral links look set to generate their own sector-specific initiatives. Meanwhile, both Basque and Welsh Governments remain committed to developing the alliance.

A Plaid Cymru Government should bring a new energy to growing and deepening such partnerships. This would establish Wales's place in the European family as well as raising our sights and finding practical solutions in economic, cultural and social development.

Recommendations

1. The Welsh Government should use the Trade and Cooperation Agreement reached between the UK and the EU at the end of 2020, to develop close bilateral relationships between Wales and the EU.

2. A Plaid Cymru Government should build upon Wales's existing International Strategy by:
   - Strengthening Wales's presence in Brussels through Wales House.
   - Developing existing partnerships with European nations and regions and examine the scope for adding to their number.

3. The Welsh Government should establish a central unit as part of the Cabinet Office to deal with international affairs and, in particular, to drive a strong and consistent policy for European engagement.

4. A Plaid Cymru Government should establish a special relationship with the EU as representing a nation aspiring to become independent and an accessor state. A priority should be to seek ways of continuing to participate in the EU Erasmus and Horizon programmes. Secondly, a Plaid Cymru Government should develop a process that puts Wales on a path towards meeting the 35 Chapters of Accession to the European Union.[71]

5. A Plaid Cymru Government should examine the scope for reaching agreement with the European Commission to enable specified products from Wales to have unfettered access to the Single Market. An inspectorate could be established to certify that products of Welsh companies participating in the scheme complied fully with EU regulations. A further possibility would be to establish a port which would export only goods in this category and where entry to the EU would be allowed without formalities.

6. In developing its relations with the European Union, a Plaid Cymru Government should pay particular attention to cultivating a close partnership with Ireland.

Relations with our neighbours: options for an independent Wales

I T IS COMMONPLACE FOR independent countries to be members of wider structures involving neighbouring countries, ranging from free-trade agreements to loose political unions such as the Nordic Union, through to confederations such as Benelux and indeed the European Union itself. In the following sections we list a number of options which we consider relevant to the potential future circumstances of an independent Wales.

These circumstances will be determined by events as they unfold over the forthcoming period, when the United Kingdom will be facing dynamic pressures that will force constitutional change. One cause is Brexit. Another is the economic instability being wrought by the Covid-19 pandemic and the Westminster Government's lamentable response. A third is the growing strength and confidence of the national movements in Wales and Scotland, together with the electoral success of Sinn Fein in Ireland.

The federal dead-end

The ground is moving beneath the feet of British unionism. This can be seen as we approach the elections in Scotland and Wales in

May 2021. In its Queen's Speech in December 2019, the newly-elected Conservative Government said it would establish a new constitution, democracy and rights commission.[72] In April 2020 the new Labour leader, Sir Keir Starmer, committed to a federal constitution, although only in aspirational terms. In an article for the *Scottish Daily Record*, he wrote:

"I want to build a future on the principle of federalism. We will establish a constitutional convention in opposition that applies that principle of federalism and a new settlement for the UK."[73]

This declaration echoed a paper 'Reforming our Union: shared governance in the UK', published by the Labour Welsh Government in October 2019. It asserts that sovereignty resides not in the Westminster Parliament but with the nations of the United Kingdom. It suggests a federal approach, and includes the following recommendations:

- The House of Lords to be replaced by a new Upper House whose membership would reflect the multinational nature of the UK rather than be population-based and which would ensure that the position of the devolved institutions are properly considered in the UK Parliament's legislation.
- Strengthening the voice of the devolved administrations in international discussions.
- Ensuring that funding be distributed among the territories in a fair, needs-based manner and that decisions on the funding of the devolved administrations should be made by a public agency which would be responsible to the four administrations jointly.
- Devolution of policing and justice to Wales.
- A Constitutional Convention to consider future constitutional developments.

Meanwhile, the cross-party House of Lords Constitutional Reform Group, chaired by the Marquis of Salisbury, has prepared an 'Act of Union Bill' which was presented formally for First Reading in the Lords in October 2019.[74] The Bill suggests a federal approach to the national territories, though that seems undermined by its retaining sovereignty with the Westminster Parliament, rather than sharing it between the different levels of government. However, the Bill's opening clauses provide for the secession of the member nations, on the basis of a simple majority in a referendum.

Indeed, this contradiction unmasks the reluctance of the English Establishment to engage on equal terms with what it still regards as the peripheral nationalities of the United Kingdom. The federal approach that is being tentatively explored is centralist in character, since it requires the maintenance of a single, undivided state.

Moreover, the size of England – with 87 per cent of the UK population – militates against a federal option. There is no federation in the world where the population of one component outstrips all the others by such a large margin. There would be no prospect of reaching a consensus between the nations of the federation on any contentious issue where England was in disagreement. As the authors of a recent study on the barriers to federalism in the UK conclude:

"Before any attempt to 'sell' the idea of Federalism to the smaller nations of the UK can even begin, there must be a desire from England for this to occur."[75]

The one practical basis on which Britain might create a federation would be if England were to first divide into regional entities – perhaps nine[76] – each having their own legislative competence. Yet, there is no impetus and very little appetite for this to happen. Politically England remains one of the most centralised states in the world. It is true that it is made up of an extraordinarily diverse and vivid pattern of regions in terms of their cultural identity. However, these have little political expression and less political representation. England is a parliamentary nation. English representation in the House of Commons is composed of a squirarchy exceedingly jealous of its entitlements and privileges, and largely contained within a two-party system that is fiercely opposed to proportional representation.

Such political regionalism that has been allowed has been confined to England's major cities – London, Birmingham and Manchester – which have been granted mayors with some executive powers. It is true that London has a representative Assembly, but it has no legislative authority that could compete with Westminster. The one serious regional initiative that was attempted was an elected Assembly for the north-east of England. But that proposal was overwhelmingly rejected in a referendum in July 2004, by 78 per cent to 22 per cent on a turn-out of 48 per cent. The No campaign was masterminded by Dominic Cummings, currently Special Adviser to Prime Minister Boris Johnson.

In a federal system powers are allocated between different, typically two, levels of government, with central government invariably being regarded as superior and the more powerful. A single constitution defines the allocation of powers.

On the other hand, confederalism is fundamentally different. Here independent, sovereign, nations voluntarily agree to delegate certain functions to a central authority, not by means of a constitution but by a treaty, with a process for unilateral withdrawal built into it. Benelux, and indeed the European Union itself, are examples.

The relationship between the member states constituting a confederation and the distribution of powers among them can vary. Nonetheless, confederalism is based on the principle of independence. Federalism is incompatible with that principle, to which Plaid Cymru is committed and which is integral to the Terms of Reference of this Commission.

Wales as a member of a confederation

Devolution involves a sovereign Westminster delegating a measure of its sovereign authority to the devolved institutions. Of course, devolution is not the same as a transfer of power. Powers that are devolved are by implication powers retained.[77]

A confederation would turn devolution on its head. It would entail four sovereign territories, of radically different population sizes (Wales 3.2m, Scotland 5.5m, Northern Ireland 1.9m, and England 56.3m) delegating some sovereign authority to central bodies in areas of agreed common interest.

A confederal approach to relationships between the nations of Britain has long been favoured by Plaid Cymru. Saunders Lewis, in his 'Principles of Nationalism', his speech to the party's first summer school in 1926, argued that we should assert our sovereignty, but only in order to be willing to share it. Similarly, in 1982 in his publication *Diwedd Prydeindod* (The End of Britishness), Gwynfor Evans argued that while Wales's future was inseparable from the rest of Britain, it needed to be framed within a new constitutional framework that provided freedom and equality for the participating nations. These, he said:

> "... would co-operate closely together in a confederation... Therefore let us ensure for Wales a place in [that kind of] partnership. That is the only worthy status for this ancient nation. Partnership is the word, for there would exist a closer relationship than is usual among its members: a warm

partnership in which each nation respects the life of the others in full."[78]

In what follows we consider two approaches to how confederal principles could be applied to a new constitutional relationship between the nations of Britain.

- The Benelux Model, as proposed by Adam Price.[79]
- A League of the Isles, as proposed by Glyndwr Cennydd Jones.[80]

Several variants could be developed on the basis of these models. It should also be emphasised that that these exemplar confederal approaches are not necessarily alternatives to independence for Wales in the EU, or as a member of European Free Trade Area (Efta) and the European Economic Area (EEA), which are explored below. An important lesson that Benelux offers us is that it is perfectly possible to be a member of a confederation which in turn operates within a wider European confederation. A confederation and membership of the European Union are therefore not mutually exclusive alternatives. Indeed, it might be argued that the changed political climate arising from the creation of such a confederation could over time encourage reintegration into the European project.

The Benelux model

In a speech in Edinburgh in June 2019, Adam Price suggested that the confederal relationship between the Netherlands, Belgium, and Luxembourg could offer a template for future relationships between the nations of Britain. As he said, it offers a completely new vision for Britain's future:

"It is one where its constituent nations come together to create a new civic sensibility and a new partnership of equals. It is one that is outward looking as well, that embraces a confident sense of being at ease with a wider sense of Europe."[81]

The Benelux confederation comprises the Netherlands (population 17.10m), Belgium (11.5m) and Luxemburg (613,000). The three countries are constitutional monarchies and Belgium is itself federated into three regions: Flanders, Wallonia and Brussels. Benelux has been described as a politico-economic union.

Benelux had its inception as a customs union established in 1949. In 1954, the Benelux Treaty of Economic Union was signed, including free movement of people, goods and services. Security, sustainable development and the economy were later added to its functions. In June 2008, a new treaty was agreed to deepen and extend the scope of collaboration, for example in education, with joint recognition of diplomas and university degrees; the police; road inspection; and adaptation to climate change. In 2018 the Benelux Youth Parliament was established.

The confederation operates through annual plans within four-yearly programmes. Five key institutions oversee the collaboration: a Parliament, a Ministerial Committee, the Benelux Council, a Court of Justice and a General Secretariat which serves all the institutions and offers assistance on organisational, diplomatic and logistical matters.

The Benelux Interparliamentary Consultative Council (established 1955) was officially renamed as the Benelux Parliament in 2019. Its task is to advise and make recommendations to the national governments on collaboration and provide information on ideas that are in circulation in the national parliaments. Its members are representatives of the national parliaments: 21 each for the Netherlands and Belgium and seven for Luxemburg.

The Ministerial Committee has four legal instruments available to it in promoting collaboration:

- Decisions, namely binding regulations that national governments must implement.
- Agreements which are presented to be ratified by individual nations.
- Recommendations which are not binding but are nevertheless very influential.
- Directives to the Council and/or the General Secretariat.

Unanimity is required among members of the Committee for these instruments to be utilised. The Benelux Council comprises chief officers of relevant ministries of the constituent nations and so its membership varies according to the subjects on the agenda. Its task is to prepare dossiers for ministers.

The Court of Justice came into force in 1974 and is composed of judges from the nations' high courts. Its task is to guarantee uniform interpretation of legal rules.

Benelux has developed an international presence through arrangements to collaborate with, for example, the Nordic Council, the Visegrad countries[82] and North Rhine-Westphalia.

Benelux is a significant example of the way in which individual countries set about collaborating across borders, ceding aspects of their independence, if not their sovereignty, in so doing. What we have here is an inter-governmental model of confederation. It is the Ministerial Committee that actually wields the power, with the Parliament fulfilling an advisory role. Membership of the institutions is based on the nations as individual entities rather than the population as citizens. The exception is the Parliament, where Luxemburg's representation is substantially smaller, and yet disproportionate to its population.

It can be seen, therefore, that Benelux operates as a sophisticated supranational structure. It has an overarching range of political, administrative and legal institutions that, taken together, constitute a relatively cohesive confederal system, operating inside the looser framework of the European Union. Yet Belgium, the

Netherlands, and even tiny Luxembourg remain distinctive, independent countries. As Adam Price concluded:

> "I would argue that by pooling their powers within both Benelux and the European Union, the three countries have enlarged and strengthened their sovereignty. By operating closely together they have obtained greater flexibility and reach in the exercise of national power, grown their economies, and enhanced their presence and prestige on the world stage."[83]

For the purposes of a confederal Britain, the Benelux model would provide for each nation to have its own sovereign parliament but with central institutions being empowered to make in many cases binding decisions which were best dealt with jointly, and make recommendations in policy areas determined by treaty.

A confederal Assembly might be established comprising representatives of the national parliaments. That Assembly might mirror the functions of the Benelux Parliament or, more ambitiously, have a role in decision-making and legislation of the kind dealt with in Benelux by the Ministerial Committee.

It should be noted, however, that what is emerging in today's UK is a process opposite to that which led to the creation of Benelux. Rather than independent countries coming together and pooling a number of important functions, what we see is nations which have had a subordinate relationship with a large neighbour over a long period of time, reasserting their desire for greater autonomy.

A League of the Isles

The League of the Isles proposal makes the case for creating a deeper, closer relationship than that suggested by Benelux. It proposes a confederation of Wales, Scotland, Northern Ireland, and England, with aspects of federal-type control built into key policy portfolios to reflect the principles of equality and solidarity shared by member nations. The Head of the Confederation continues to be the British monarch. Each nation has a distinct jurisdiction and holds all constitutional powers and rights which are not by treaty delegated to joint institutions.

The constituent parts of a League of the Isles would be as follows.

Council of The Isles

The Council of the Isles has mechanisms to address the asymmetry between population sizes of the member nations, specifically through the composition and distribution of seats. Members of the Council are typically elected for a four-year period by the electors of each nation, convening annually for a fixed time unless urgent business is demanded. The Council assumes its own standing orders, confirming a Presiding Officer and Executive whose Prime Minister and Ministers are responsible for defence, foreign policy, internal trade, currency, macro-economic policy, and isle-wide affairs.

In advance of final reading, each Bill considered by the Council is circulated to the National Parliaments of Wales, Scotland, Northern Ireland, and England, with member nations empowered to make objections or suggest amendments before voting. This provides a counterweight to any tendency of the centre to aggregate power within its core, and to act unilaterally on matters such as defence and foreign affairs. Once passed, the Head of the Confederation confirms the Bill as an Act of the Council of the Isles. The ultimate authority on the legitimacy of any law and treaty remains with the Supreme Court.

Committee of Member Nations

A Committee of Member Nations (comprising the Council's Prime Minister and Minister for Isle-wide Affairs, and the First Minister of each member nation), convenes regularly to discuss more general considerations which demand a degree of co-operation and harmonisation of laws across borders, over and above the key functions enacted in Council. These include: postal, telephonic and internet communications; railways, roads and associated licensing; airports, ports and traffic controls; coastguard and navigational services; energy, water and related infrastructure; income and corporation taxes; rates of sales, weights and measures; copyrights, patents and trademarks; scientific and technological research; broadcasting; meteorological forecasting; environmental protection; civil defence; emergencies, and the prevention of terrorism and serious crime.

The Committee, with support of the Council, also holds controls for confirming contractual-type arrangements for supplying any public services to member nations, if requested. To cover the common functions and agreements in place, the Council levies charges upon each member nation according to a defined proportion of their GDP relative to that of the confederation as a whole. These monies are paid annually into a consolidated fund from which the interest on the UK public debt continues as a standing charge. The League aims to promote equality across the isles by sharing a measure of baseline investment for infrastructure projects, operating formal instruments for resolving disagreements. National Parliaments are discouraged from misusing any advantages they possess in areas of potential contention including, for example, the economy of England, the oil of Scotland, and the water of Wales. Some central responsibility is also assigned for pensions and what were previously termed National Insurance contributions (appropriately renamed), mitigating elements of financial risk and promoting ongoing solidarity. Further, federal-type mechanisms may be introduced to support fiscal decentralisation from the UK position.

National Parliaments

The National Parliament of each member nation sits as the sovereign, legislative and representative body of its people, enacting powers and laws on every issue that is not identified as within the Council's remit. A Government is appointed which has the support of a majority of the nation's parliamentary members, comprising a First Minister and other ministerial positions as required to oversee the various departments. The superior judges are nominated on the advice of an independent authority. Nations further sub-divide their lands through Acts of National Parliament, defining the composition and responsibilities of local or regional authorities.

Overview

In overview, within a model of a League of the Isles:

- Citizens elect representatives to their respective National Parliament and a central Council of the Isles, relating to their member nation, initially, and to the League next, and with equal rights of movement, residence, and employment in all nations.
- The Council levies charges upon each member nation according to a defined proportion of their GDP annually. Aspects of federal-type co-ordination support fiscal decentralisation away from the current UK arrangements, with the nations operating distinct tax regimes unless centrally assigned, and with borrowing monitored. There is a common currency and a central Bank of the Isles.
- Each nation holds all powers which are not delegated to the centre. The Council enacts clearly defined authority

on matters involving defence, foreign policy, internal trade, currency, large-scale economics, and isle-wide affairs. A Committee of Member Nations promotes co-operation across borders. The right to secession from the centre is implicit in the model as sovereignty rests with the nations.

- Each nation operates its own legal jurisdiction. A Supreme Court of the Isles judges on any dispute concerning powers between member nations.
- The League's nations independently hold seats at the UN General Assembly.

Imponderables

The Benelux and League of the Isles models illustrate variants of possible co-operation within a confederal partnership. Whatever model is adopted, the powers delegated to the centre will necessarily balance competing priorities. On the one hand, the member nations will desire to promote their own interests and implement policies that accord with their particular political traditions. On the other, they will wish to co-operate on common functions for the benefit of all the member nations in a spirit of solidarity. The latter would include the following benefits:

- Making decisions in common where they can best be progressed jointly.
- Discouraging the implementation of policies by one country to the detriment of one or more of the others.
- Sharing risks.
- Gaining economies of scale.

The Independence Commission's deliberations are being conducted at a time of rapid and unpredictable political change. We note that Adam Price's 'Seven Steps to Independence' sets out a process of 'nation building' leading to an independence referendum by 2030.[84] Granted a Yes vote, there would then follow a negotiated departure from the existing UK which could take, say, two years. Thus, an independent Wales would come into existence in 2032. Entry into the EU, if that were the preferred route, would probably take at least a further four years, bringing us to 2036.

Adam Price's paper allows for an earlier referendum depending on other political developments, but for the moment let us consider the 'unknowns' that relate to that time-frame.

One of those is the evolution of the European Union, which we have considered in the previous chapter. Suffice it to say at this point that there will be an active debate between those favouring further integration and those wanting to reassert the powers of the nation–states, with various versions in between.

The second is the future political complexion of the UK and particularly England. Despite the impact of the Covid-19 pandemic on the public finances, with major increases in public expenditure, the trend towards neoliberal exceptionalism represented by the present Conservative leadership may be consolidated. In that case a so-called 'globalised' UK would drift further apart from continental Europe and enter the orbit of the USA. However, this is by no means certain. The realities of the international scene may cause the UK to realise that its optimum destiny lies in a close relationship with its near neighbours in Europe. At the same time domestic political opinion may shift towards favouring a more social democratic government.

A third unknown is the future of Northern Ireland which voted to remain in the EU in the 2016 referendum. In order to seal a departure agreement, the UK was obliged to agree to maintaining an open border between the Republic and Northern Ireland at the cost of establishing a new customs border in the Irish Sea. Northern Ireland will therefore be a part of the EU single market, along with the Republic. This new factor could well expedite the establishment of a United Ireland.

The fourth unknown, highly relevant to the Welsh situation, is the political future of Scotland.

The SNP is determined that there be a second referendum on Scottish independence and its demand seems likely to be endorsed by the electors in the May 2021 Holyrood election. We understand that the Scottish Government is currently preparing in detail for negotiations, following a presumed Yes vote, for accession to the EU. As far as the SNP Government is concerned, consideration of the nature of any future intra-British relationship is very much on the back-burner.

The constitutional power to allow an independence referendum lies with the British Government. This is, in our view, unacceptable. Decisions on the constitutional future of Scotland and Wales should lie unequivocally with the peoples of those nations. However, the present reality is that Scottish entry as an independent country into the EU is dependent on any referendum being strictly constitutional. The UK Government is not at present inclined to allow such a referendum, a stance that is likely to trigger a constitutional crisis and strengthen the pro-independence movement. It is likely, as well, that at some point the UK Government will be obliged to relent, certainly if the SNP was victorious at the next UK parliamentary election, scheduled for November 2024. Let us then assume, therefore, that an independence referendum is held in 2025.

There will then be negotiations for Scotland's departure from the UK, which could take up to two years. As to EU membership, it has been argued that "the fastest... Scotland might join the EU is 4-5 years from independence".[85] If that is the case, the earliest an independent Scotland could become a member of the EU is in 2031-2. An issue relevant to those negotiations would be the extent of the UK's (and therefore

Scotland's) divergence from European regulations after departure at the end of 2020.

However, a means of dealing with this last problem has been suggested. This would involve Scotland and the EU agreeing a comprehensive pre-accession agreement. It would provide "a mechanism of dynamic alignment that would minimise divergence between Scotland and the EU even if the period until membership is longer than expected."[86] During that period an independent Scotland, through associate EEA membership, would be within the single market.

Without such an agreement Scotland would remain within a UK single market and customs union. In that case, it would probably, perhaps inevitably, retain sterling and thus be subject to monetary policy determined by the Bank of England. The nature of the relationship between Scotland and the rest of the UK, including any institutional arrangements, would have been discussed during the departure negotiations at which the Welsh Government should be present.

At some stage during this lengthy and intricate process (and some would say that the time-frame outlined above is optimistic) an offer of a federal Britain as an alternative to Scottish independence, and with a view to 'saving the union', will in all probability be made. As stated earlier, the House of Lords Constitutional Reform Group (CRG) is currently working on a detailed proposal with its Act of Union Bill, a revised version of which is to appear before the end of 2020.[87]

Federalism, as we have argued above, would in our view be an unsatisfactory compromise for a number of reasons. Based as it is on a constitution determined centrally, it is incompatible with the notion of independent nations agreeing voluntarily to delegate certain functions to the centre (although the CRG Act of Union Bill seeks to square this circle by providing for the unilateral secession of the constituent nations). In our view, asserting the national sovereignty of Wales and Scotland through independence is the only way of modifying, if not eliminating, the dominance of England in any new arrangements.

A Yes vote in a Scottish referendum would unlock the situation so as to allow a comprehensive debate about a new relationship between the independent nations on the island of Britain. That is why, earlier in this chapter, we have explored options around a confederal approach. They may offer improbable scenarios at present, given the Scottish Government's pressure for an independence referendum and the Westminster Government's intransigence in refusing to countenance one. However, as events unfold, with both sides eventually having to concede the benefits of constructive co-existence on our shared island, a confederal approach might become seen as attractive.

It is against this background that we now consider the options for an independent Wales in terms of its relationship with the rest of Europe.

Wales as a member of the European Union

Full membership of the EU has been a key part of Plaid Cymru's programme for more than 30 years. The UK's departure from the EU has changed the picture, increasing the support for independence, while possibly making it more problematic at the same time.

The attitudes that led to Brexit spring from a neo-liberal ideology combined with a sense of English exceptionalism, by now deeply ingrained in the dominant faction of the Conservative Party. The difficulty for Wales is that as long as this set of attitudes and policies persists, the possibility of our escaping as an independent nation into the far more compatible embrace of the European Union is made more difficult.

The reason is that for over many centuries Wales's economy

has been closely integrated into that of England. The development of a west–east road and rail network at the expense of an internal one, particularly between north and south, a deliberate act of policy, has contributed to this. Inevitably, however, the proximity of England has made it a hugely significant market for Welsh products. Some 60 per cent of Wales's external trade is with the rest of the UK, mainly England.[88] Equally, Wales relies to a very great extent on imports from or via England. There are some 480 crossing points at the border and roughly 150,000 people cross it daily to work, as well as for leisure and medical care.

Were Wales to become an independent EU member-state the Wales–England border would also be the EU–England border. It is the EU therefore that would negotiate the kind of agreement necessary to enable free and unfettered trade across that border, although it would, of course, do so in close consultation with the Welsh Government. The EU has demonstrated in the case of Ireland its solidarity with small member-states by obliging the UK to allow unfettered trade across the border between the Republic and Northern Ireland. Of course, that has entailed creating a customs border in the Irish Sea in order to protect the integrity of the European Single Market. There is no such option available in the case of the Wales–England border.

Therefore, as long as the UK Government remains obdurate in its determination to detach Britain, commercially as well as politically, from mainland Europe, it is hard to see how an independent Wales could, separately from England, become a member of the EU.

Wales as a member of the European Free Trade Area

However, a further option might be for an independent Wales to seek membership of the European Free Trade Area (Efta), with a view to becoming part of the European Economic Area (EEA). Efta comprises Norway, Iceland, Liechtenstein, and Switzerland.

The EEA was established by an international treaty entered into by the 'Contracting Parties', namely the EU, each member state of the EU in its own right, plus Norway, Iceland and Liechtenstein. The EEA is an enlarged single market that embraces the EU and has 500 million consumers. Its members generate 25 per cent of global GDP. Moreover, it accounts for 44 per cent of UK exports and 57 per cent of UK imports. Membership of the EEA would give Wales free and unfettered access to this Single Market.

While Efta is not a customs union and its member states have full rights to enter into bilateral third-country trade arrangements, it does have a co-ordinated trade policy. Efta members jointly negotiate with third countries whenever possible. In practice Efta members have negotiated free trade agreements with most of those third countries with whom the EU has free trade agreements.

Membership of the EEA confers membership of the EU single market. EEA members pay an amount – negotiated with the EU – for access. Membership of the single market means that EEA states align their regulatory standards with those of the EU. This alignment means that EEA workers, services, goods and capital can move freely in the territory of the EU and the EEA. There are institutional arrangements which give EEA member states the right to influence the content of EU single market measures, though no vote in the EU institutions. However, unlike EU member states, EU single market measures in EEA states do not have a direct effect. There is also some scope for EEA states to implement EU single market measures more flexibly. EEA member states are also not under EU scrutiny. There is a separate body (the Efta surveillance commission) which oversees compliance with EEA measures and a separate judicial body (the Efta court), on which there would be a Welsh judge, which gives rulings on EEA legal issues.

As a member of Efta, Wales would be permitted to negotiate free-trade agreements with third countries. In principle, therefore, as a member of Efta an independent Wales would be in a position, in its own right, to negotiate a free-trade agreement with England. As an EEA member Wales would have to comply with EEA/EU standards. Imports from England into Wales would also have to comply with those standards. However it would, in principle, be permissible to allow imports from England at low or no tariffs provided that they were not re-exported to the EU.

Welsh exporters to England would have to comply with English standards but, certainly on present form, those would be unlikely to be more onerous than EEA/EU standards. Certainly, it would be in the mutual interests of Wales and England to arrive at a comprehensive free-trade agreement.

Whereas Efta might welcome into its ranks a small country eager to develop close links with Europe, there might well be obstacles to Welsh membership. One can anticipate a degree of goodwill towards Wales, but the EEA would need to be satisfied that its own free and unfettered access to the EU single market would not be imperilled by:

(i)   issues arising from the permeability of the Wales–England border; or

(ii) any divergence from EU standards.

The EU itself would keep a close eye on the negotiations and probably insist on input to them. It should also be noted that Wales, being outside the political structures of the EU, would have no place at the decision-making table.

The Efta and EEA option opens interesting possibilities for an independent Wales, not least as an eventual route back into the EU, but it is by no means straightforward. The statutory National Commission which a Plaid Cymru government should establish following the May 2021 Senedd election should conduct an in-depth exploration of this option and associated matters.

At this point it is worth raising the question of how long the UK, dominated as it is by England, will continue to maintain its present antipathy to the European Union. As the reality of failing to gain unfettered access to European markets begins to dawn on the people of Britain and their political class, it is not unimaginable that common sense will prevail and that the UK will, over time, see the need for a return to at least a close economic relationship with the European Union.

It is asking too much for this to take the form of renewed EU membership. And, indeed, if an application were made it is by no means certain, following the chaotic disruption of the last four years, that it would be welcomed. However, a relationship that allowed unfettered access to the Single Market involving close regulatory alignment and a removal of customs barriers might be another matter. Certainly, the Trade and Cooperation Agreement reached at the end of 2020 holds out the prospect of that eventually happening.

In those circumstances the road would be open for an independent Wales to enter the EU as a member-state. That, in our view, should remain the ultimate objective for an independent Wales, with joining Efta a possible interim step. In the meanwhile, there are other ways of nurturing a relationship with the EU as part of the intention for Wales to grow into being a mature European nation. These have been explored in Chapter 7.

The way ahead

In present circumstances it seems to us that the interests of Wales, and the growing aspiration for independence, would be best served within the framework of a confederation. The close links that Wales and Scotland have over many centuries formed with England make the case for a radically changed relationship between our three nations, rather than complete separation.

This does not alter our view that Wales's national interests would also be best served by eventually rejoining the European Union. We have referred to the challenges that Wales would have to face in seeking EU membership separately from England. Efta and EEA membership may be an option. These also involve challenges which are real but may not be insurmountable.

It is evident that a confederation is only possible with the participation of Scotland. Such participation would not, in our view, mean that Scotland, any more than Wales, would have to set aside its aspiration to become a fully-fledged member of the EU. On the contrary, we suggest that the creation of a confederation would, in fact, offer an alternative route back into Europe. That route would be available for each of the confederation's nations to seek accession to the EU, when circumstances are favourable.

Alternatively, the confederation, acting through its constituent nations, could seek membership of Efta and then become part of the EEA. That would place it in a deep and close association with the EU and thus the wider European project as well.

Any successful moves to creating the kind of confederation we have outlined, would in themselves contribute to creating a new political climate in which the route back to Europe would be made more likely

Recommendations

1. Plaid Cymru should retain its commitment to an independent Wales becoming a member of the European Union.

2. Federalism, being promoted by elements within the UK unionist parties as an alternative to Welsh and Scottish independence, is impractical since England comprises 87 per cent of the UK population, while there is no plan or desire to divide England into regional territories, particularly with legislative powers.

3. The statutory National Commission should conduct discussions with the Scottish Government with a view to arriving at a consensus on future relations and structures between the nations of Britain.

4. The statutory National Commission should establish contacts with Benelux in order to consider the applicability of its confederal model to a reconstituted Britain, recognising that Belgium, Netherlands and Luxembourg are members of the EU.

5. The statutory National Commission should conduct an examination into which policy fields might be delegated to the centre within a confederation such as outlined in the Benelux and League of the Isles models.

6. By pooling aspects of their sovereignty in a confederal relationship, the countries of Britain have an opportunity to achieve a more evenly-distributed, and hence improved, economic performance. If they do so at the same time as furthering relations with the European Union they also have an opportunity to enhance their presence and prestige on the world stage.

7. The statutory National Commission should examine the possibility of Wales, separately from England, joining Efta and the EEA.

CHAPTER 8

A Constitution for an independent Wales

THIS CHAPTER SETS OUT the legal issues which need to be resolved before a pathway to establishing a Welsh Constitution can be mapped out. It also provides recommendations for the shape of a constitution based on the views of the members of the Commission.

A constitution is of central importance to the life of any independent state, and its drafting entails many complex and detailed issues. It cannot be stressed too strongly, therefore, that the Elements of a Welsh Constitution explored in this chapter can only be the starting point of a consultation process in which everyone in Wales needs to be involved.

Principles of a Welsh Constitution

The first principle is that the path to an independent Wales with its own constitution should be a constitutional one. It should be achieved by a series of steps, the legality of which should be clear, and the provisions of which would therefore be recognised and enforced by public servants, including the judiciary, not only within Wales but in other jurisdictions.

Other starting points for the Welsh Constitution recommended by the Commission include the following:

- A declaration that Welsh sovereignty rests with the people of Wales.
- That it should include a description and role of Welsh governing institutions as well as the rights and responsibilities of citizens.
- That those rights and responsibilities should extend beyond the purely political and legalistic to encompass social and economic rights and responsibilities.
- That it should draw on best practice from around the world, especially constitutions that have been drawn up for small nations in analogous positions to that of Wales.

First, some basic concepts on which a constitution for an independent Wales should rest, need to be made clear.

Independence

By 'independence' (otherwise known as 'sovereignty') we mean a state of affairs in which a political community (a 'state') is not subject to legal control by any other state. Such external legal constraints on its activities as exist are imposed, not by the suzerainty of another state but by treaty obligations which it has freely entered into and from which it can, upon giving due notice, withdraw.

The unique significance of the status of independent state is illustrated by the fact that it is the basis of full membership of all international organisations and of the ability to enter into treaty relations with other similar communities. Articles 3 and 4 of the Charter of the United Nations specifically restrict membership of the United Nations to 'states' and Article 2(1) embraces "the principle of the sovereign equality" of all its member states.

The original member states of the UN when it was established in 1945 numbered 51 and represented almost all existing sovereign states at that time, other than those such as Germany and Japan, whose involvement in the recently concluded war, or their lack of functioning government, excluded them from membership for the time being. By the beginning of 2020 the number of member states had grown to 193, largely due to the process of decolonisation under which a number of European states, most prominently the United Kingdom and France, had relinquished control over overseas territories in Africa, Asia and the Caribbean. The territories in question advanced, as a result, to independence, enabling them to apply to become members of the UN.

A legal process by which a territory which had not previously been independent achieves that status has therefore been a prominent and well-precedented feature of constitutional practice over the past 75 years, not least within the former British empire.

Constitution

By a 'constitution', lawyers generally mean a set of rules which govern the internal workings of the state. These rules define who has the power, within the state, to make laws which are binding on citizens and what procedures must be followed when doing so. They delineate the functions of different specialised organs of the state (usually classified as legislature, executive and judiciary) and define how the individuals who exercise the functions of those institutions (parliamentarians, ministers, judges) are chosen.

By definition, every state has a constitution. No political community can function without the kind of rules referred to in the last paragraph. But the form that these rules take – in other words, the form of the constitution – differs widely.

In keeping with ideas of order and logic which originated in the Age of Enlightenment, states, almost without exception, have chosen to incorporate at least the most important rules of their constitutions into a single comprehensive document – commonly referred to as 'the Constitution' – and to mark the importance of such rules by requiring them to be adopted and, if necessary amended, in accordance with special procedures. These (for example, the need for a special majority in the legislature or for ratification by the electorate in a referendum) are specifically designed to make it more difficult to amend constitutional rules than to make ordinary laws. The aim is to protect the fundamental structures and workings of the state from being altered for short-term political gain by transitory political forces. We refer to the protection of constitutional rules in this way as 'entrenchment'.

Common (although not universal) features of codified constitutions are statements of basic constitutional principles (such as that of the sovereignty of the people, the rule of law and democracy) and of fundamental individual, collective, civic or, nowadays, social, economic or environmental rights (a 'Bill of Rights').

As it happens, the United Kingdom is one of the handful of states which has not, so far, chosen to adopt a codified, entrenched constitution, although there are of course many rules of law, both statutory and customary, whose content is 'constitutional'. Examples of constitutional legislation are the Fixed Term Parliaments Act 2011 and the Wales Act 2017. But the absence of a single, codified constitution, having a higher legal status than that of other legislation, means that there is no vehicle for statements of general constitutional principles nor of any meaningful Bill of Rights. It also gives rise to two characteristic features of the UK constitution which are increasingly seen as anachronistic.

Firstly, UK laws that deal with constitutional matters have no higher status than that of any other law. A law to curb the powers of the House of Lords could, as a matter of constitutional law, be enacted according to exactly the same procedure as a law to put an extra penny in the pound on income tax. The ability of the UK Parliament to change the law is not, and in the absence of any overarching collection of constitutional rules can never be, constrained by any superior rules. Put another way, Parliament (in practice the House of Commons), as the law-making body at a UK level, is supreme.

Secondly, in the absence of any codified UK constitution, there is no clear definition of which matters need to be governed by law and which can be left to custom and practice. This has resulted in the proliferation of 'constitutional conventions', that is rules that do not have the force of law but operate on the basis of an assumption that they represent established practice. Important rules to do with issues such as the powers of ministers, the extent of Royal prerogative (that is, non-statutory) powers and the choice of a Prime Minister when no single party has a majority in the House of Commons, are governed not by laws but by ill-defined conventions which, in the event of a novel situation arising or a decision by the executive to defy convention, cannot be defined with certainty, let alone enforced effectively.

Lawyers from the continental civil law tradition (as opposed to that of Anglo-American common law) have a different understanding of what is meant by a constitution. For civil lawyers, a constitution is the fundamental law of the state. All other domestic laws derive their authority from being made in accordance with it, both in the sense of having been made according to the methods prescribed by the constitution for law-making (the common lawyer's understanding of the concept), but also in the sense of being consonant with the principles which are enshrined in it. A constitution in this sense is not simply those laws which govern the workings of the state powers. It is the fundamental law of the state in all matters. In this sense, the United Kingdom does not have a constitution although it has constitutional laws. It is not just that it has no written constitution; it has no fundamental law from which all other laws derive their validity and from which every public authority derives its legitimacy.

Such constitutions are likely to include a clear statement that sovereignty belongs to the people, followed by certain guarantees of fundamental rights which the people are to enjoy on an equal basis. Some of these rights will pertain to individuals, others to groups. Some of the rights will be political or civil in character, others economic, social or moral. The constitution will also provide for mechanisms by which laws protect and enforce those rights against other persons and against the state itself, and to provide for the punishment of those who infringe the protected rights of others. Some such constitutions go so far as to define the purpose for which the state which they govern exists. If such a statement occurs, it will probably formulate the function of the state as being to protect the individual and possibly the family and to promote the common good. It will probably also commit the state to doing this by protecting such basic values as liberty, equality, security, peace and the development of the individual as a person.

Some of these functions of a constitution set aims rather than describe current achievements. They commit the state to pursuing goals which may not be immediately capable of full realisation, for example, goals relating to health, education and employment. These goals are aspirational, but their presence within the constitution commits the state to their pursuit, and policies or laws which hinder or contradict their achievement will be open to challenge as a consequence of the constitutional status of the goals in question. Without such an enhanced status, it is difficult to accommodate aspirational goals in legislation effectively, as arguably is proving the case, for instance, in relation to those of the Senedd's Well-being of Future Generations (Wales) Act 2015.

Other, more immediately operative, functions require that the state constantly gives effect to the protection guaranteed by the constitution. This it will do by legislating to facilitate and/or protect the rights in question. Thus, for example, the constitution may recognise a right to peaceful enjoyment of property. This will obligate the state to legislate to provide for legal means by which persons may acquire property, transfer it by gift or sale, succeed to it on the death of a previous owner, secure it against the interests of others, recover it from others if it is lost, obtain compensation from others if it is damaged or destroyed, and by which those who wrongfully interfere with the property rights of others can be punished for crimes such as theft. These issues will be dealt with in ordinary legislation, but the state is obligated to make such provision. In civil law countries, the relevant rules will be found in their Civil Code and Criminal Code, together with enforcement mechanisms in the Codes of Civil and Criminal Procedure. But the content of these codes, as well as the mechanism by which they are enacted, derive their validity from the Constitution.

The minimum content of a Welsh Constitution

As the example of the United Kingdom demonstrates, there is no absolute necessity for a state to have a codified, entrenched constitution. Nevertheless, the absence of such a document underpinning the functioning of government in the UK and in particular the virtually untrammelled power that it places in the hands of a Prime Minister who has a commanding majority in the House of Commons, has given rise to increasing concern.

The Commission is of the view, therefore that, as a very minimum, the constitution of an independent Wales should incorporate:

- A statement of basic principles on which the state is founded, required to be upheld by everyone exercising powers under the constitution.
- A statement of fundamental rights and freedoms.
- Definition of the powers of the main elements of the state and of the ways in which they relate to one another.

- Machinery for amendment of the constitution (whatever its form) which effectively entrenches the main elements of the constitution, including the fundamental rights which it guarantees.

The obvious means by which these minimum requirements could be met would be by the enactment of a codified Welsh Constitution.

In May 2021, under the terms of the Legislation (Wales) Act 2019, the incoming Welsh Government will be under a duty to prepare a programme to improve the accessibility of Welsh law by, among other things, an ongoing process of consolidation and codification. This programme must thereafter initiate and maintain a codified form of Welsh law. This trend in Welsh law is consistent with the concept of a constitution, being a fundamental law in the civil law sense from which the other codified areas of the law will derive validity in terms of their substantive content as well as their process of enactment.

Pathway to a Welsh Constitution

The following stages can be identified as necessary to the achievement of a Welsh Constitution:

(i) An Act of the UK Parliament preparing for and accepting the ending of UK sovereignty over Wales.

(ii) An Act of the Senedd establishing a process leading to the adoption of a Welsh Constitution.

(iii) The implementation of that process, culminating in the coming into force of that Constitution.

1. Termination of Westminster sovereignty

The existence of a Welsh legislature, Senedd Cymru, makes the initial step of releasing sovereignty to Wales a relatively straightforward one from a legal point of view. Section 107 of the Government of Wales Act 2006 confers on the Senedd the general power to make laws in relation to Wales, but the Act then goes on to qualify that power in a number of ways:

- It preserves a residual right for Westminster to make laws for Wales if it chooses (s107(5) and (6)).
- It specifies (section108A) certain subjects on which the Senedd may not legislate (the 'reserved matters' set out in Schedule 7A together with the restrictions set out in Schedule 7B).
- It now sets out further reservations specific to 'retained EU law' (section 109A).

The core of any 'Wales (Independence) Act' would therefore be a repeal of all those provisions in the Government of Wales Act 2006 which reserve to Westminster the power to legislate on any matters in relation to Wales. The 2006 Act would thereby become Wales's interim constitution.

Not all restrictions on the power of the Senedd to legislate would need to be removed at this stage. The substance of the prohibition on making laws that are incompatible with the European Convention on Human Rights might well be retained, although it would need to be directly referable to the European Convention itself rather than the UK Human Rights Act 1998. And although the restrictions on amending the Government of Wales Act 2006 itself would need to cease, the requirement for a super-majority (support of two-thirds of the membership of the Senedd) for legislation dealing with matters of fundamental constitutional importance, such as the number of Members of the Senedd and how they are elected, could be retained, entrenching Wales's temporary constitution.

The only new element that would need to be incorporated into the Independence Act would be the provision of alternative machinery for exercising the functions of the Crown in Wales (for example, assenting to Acts and appointing the First Minister).

Normal practice would be to create a new office of Governor or, more appropriate to the modern world, that of a Crown Commissioner. This would enable the functions of the Head of State in Wales to be exercised, at least until the enactment of a Welsh Constitution, in the name of the Queen but by a citizen of Wales.

2. Transition to an independent Wales

Legislation to give effect to Welsh independence would need to include a number of important transitional provisions, including:

- The definition of Welsh citizenship.
- The rights of Welsh and UK citizens in the other country (for example, through the mutual recognition of citizenship rights in the same way as was achieved in relation to Ireland by the Ireland Act 1949). Similar arrangements would be needed in relation to the position of Irish and Commonwealth citizens in Wales.
- Provision regarding the retention and continuation of law applying to Wales prior to independence.
- Creation of an independent Welsh public service.
- Transfer of civil and public servants in Wales to the Welsh state.
- Transfer of office holders (including judges) to the Welsh state.
- Division of obligations (including pension rights) relating to present and past public servants between Wales and the continuing UK.
- Division of other assets and liabilities (and the allocation of contractual rights and duties under continuing contracts) between Wales and the continuing UK (or England, depending on the status of Scotland and Northern Ireland).

- Provision for the continuing operation of cross-border public services (for example the north-south borders railway line).
- Provision with regard to continuing rights and obligations under existing treaties and the future of defence and national security interests.

The practical complexity of some of these issues would be considerable and they would almost certainly need to be referred to a joint commission with the power to agree and enforce the details of whatever arrangements they made in particular cases.

3. Process for the drafting and adoption of a Welsh Constitution

The adoption by an existing state of a new constitution requires a process by which the new constitution is drafted, approved and adopted.

Practice relating to the drafting of a constitution varies. The government of the state may take the initiative and instruct its lawyers to produce a draft, in accordance with the government's vision of what it should contain, submitting it to processes of public consultation before arriving at a final draft. Alternatively, legislation may establish an independent body, representing a range of interests and views and including members with relevant expertise, to supervise the drafting of the constitution.

Legislation would certainly be required in order to regulate the processes of approval and adoption of a draft. Approval might be by a body specially created for that sole purpose – a 'constitutional assembly' or 'convention'. Alternatively, the draft might be considered by the legislature in the same way as it considers other forms of legislation. In either case there would need to be the opportunity for the approving body to scrutinise and to amend the draft before finally approving it.

Final adoption of the constitution invariably requires a procedure which differs from that which applies to the enactment of ordinary legislation, reflecting the superior legal status of a constitution. This could involve a requirement for a special majority (typically two-thirds) in the legislature and/or final submission of the approved draft for adoption by popular vote in a referendum or plebiscite.

Elements of a Welsh Constitution

The following summarises the Commission's views as to what elements should be included in the constitution of an independent Wales. It does not purport to include every detail which would need to be included in the constitution, let alone to specify the precise wording of the document. For example, a key feature of a Welsh Constitution should be a firm and clear commitment to the principle of sustainability, as currently enshrined in the ground-breaking Well-being of Future Generations (Wales) Act 2015. But the form of that commitment calls for careful and detailed discussion so as to build further on the foundations laid by that legislation.

The precise details of the constitution would need to be discussed and agreed by the people of Wales and their representatives. This would be necessary to achieve the level of consensus and certainty which are essential if a constitution is to fulfil its purpose as the basic law of the state. Nevertheless, what follows represents an outline of the kind of Wales which could be achieved were Wales to be independent and, as such, is a basis on which a Welsh Constitution could be based.

Founding principles

The constitution, which is the basic law which gives legitimacy to all state powers, should explicitly declare that it is based on the principle of *popular sovereignty*. Adoption of the constitution would be a collective decision by the people of Wales to transfer to the state certain defined and limited powers over their lives, in the interests of the common good. It should further be made clear that this acceptance by the people of limits on their individual freedom is conditional on respect by the state of certain *basic principles* (to be defined further in the Bill of Rights) namely:

- Democracy.
- Subsidiarity – that is, the principle that actions by the state can only be justified in order to achieve desirable social outcomes that cannot be achieved as effectively by individual efforts, and that such actions should always be taken at the most local level compatible with the effective achievement of the outcomes in question.
- The Rule of Law.
- Equality of all people.
- Individual and collective freedom (constrained only by such laws as are essential in a democratic society for the protection of the freedom of others).
- Sustainability (that is, the principle that the needs of the present are to be met without harming the well-being of future generations by compromising the ability of those generations to meet their own needs).

The identity of the state

Name: The Constitution should define the name of the state as 'Cymru' or, in the English language, 'Wales'.

Languages: Welsh and English should be accorded the status of official languages of the state. In all their dealings with the state (including with all public bodies and local authorities) those who wish to use either of the official languages are entitled to do so without discrimination. The legal equality of the two official languages:

- Does not affect the ability of public authorities to take positive measures to foster and facilitate greater use of the Welsh language.
- Does not prevent action encouraging other linguistic groups to maintain and develop their own historic languages and cultures.
- Does not affect the duty of public authorities to take all steps necessary to ensure that they can communicate effectively with residents who are members of such groups.

Flag: Y Ddraig Goch should be recognised by the constitution as the flag of the state.

Citizenship: Citizenship of Wales should be open to all those permanently resident in Wales (even if temporarily absent) at the date of independence and should thereafter be automatically acquired by all those born in Wales. Legislation should define further categories of citizen, including children born to Welsh citizens temporarily resident outside Wales, those taking up permanent residence in Wales (after a period long enough to demonstrate a commitment to Welsh citizenship) and to persons of Welsh descent able to demonstrate a sufficiently close practical connection with Wales (for example, the children of recent emigrants). Citizenship should not, however, be the test of the right to vote in Wales – this should be open to all permanent residents of Wales.

A Welsh Bill of Rights: The Constitution should contain a statement of those fundamental rights and freedoms (a Bill of Rights) to which the state is required to give effect, not only by its own direct actions but through a framework of laws binding on private individuals and organisations. These should fall into four categories:

- Traditional individual and civic rights of the kind contained in the European Convention for the Protection of Human Rights and Political Freedoms (ECHR). These should, as under the Human Rights Act 1998 at present, be made part of domestic Welsh law, by incorporating the Convention into the Constitution and providing that any failure by a public body to give effect to these rights is to be actionable in the courts.

- A Charter of linguistic, religious, ethnic and cultural rights (for example, the right to use either of the two languages without discrimination when dealing with public bodies) which would also be directly enforceable in the courts.
- A Charter of economic and environmental rights (including the right to a safe environment) to which public bodies would be obliged to give effect, failing which their acts or failures to act would be open to challenge in the courts. The precise content of these rights and the means by which they could be enforced would need to be the subject of careful and inclusive discussion.
- A Charter safeguarding the rights of future generations in accordance with the principles currently enshrined in the Well-being of Future Generations (Wales) Act 2015 – but strengthened, simplified and made applicable to both public and private sectors. The Charter would require all concerned to take account, in their actions, of the long-term impact of their decisions and to require those decisions to involve working with people, communities and others with a view to eliminating persistent problems such as poverty, health inequalities and climate change.

Forms and institutions of government

The basic form of the state, as defined in the Constitution, would be that of a parliamentary democracy in which executive powers are exercised by a government answerable to the parliament and which holds office only so long as it enjoys the confidence of a majority of the members of the parliament. The making and revision of laws would be the exclusive function of the parliament as legislature (except to the extent that it had delegated the power to make law to others – for example, by empowering the making by ministers of subordinate legislation. The power of the parliament to make laws would not, however, be unfettered. Such laws would need to be consistent with the Constitution, including the Bill of Rights and this standard would be enforced by an independent, non-political, judiciary.

The Head of State

The main functions of the Head of State would be:

- To uphold the Constitution.
- To be the formal representative of the state in its relations with other states – so that treaties would, for example, be signed in the name of the Head of State although they would require ratification by the parliament.
- To assent to Bills passed by the parliament, upon which they would become law.
- To make appointments to key public offices (ministers, judges, ombudsmen, commissioners, ambassadors) in accordance with the relevant processes for identifying the appropriate candidate (for example, nomination by the parliament in the case of a First Minister or recommendation by the judicial appointments commission in the case of judges).
- To be the formal head of the armed forces (although these would normally act in accordance with the directions of the government).
- The Head of State would have no executive powers as such. The government would be answerable to the parliament not to the Head of State. The Head of State would not, therefore, be head of the executive arm of

government as in the case of the United States of America or of France. From a practical point of view, the role of Head of State could equally well be discharged by a truly constitutional hereditary monarch (as in the case of Norway or Denmark), or by an elected President (as in the case of Ireland or Finland). If it were decided to retain the current UK monarchy, but within the framework of a Welsh constitution, the powers of the monarch would need to be delegated to a locally-based representative who would be a Welsh citizen, as is the case with the Governors-General of independent Commonwealth territories such as New Zealand and Canada, although a title such as Crown Commissioner would seem to be more fitting than Governor-General, with its echoes of Empire.

• The practical functional difference between a republic headed by an elected non-executive President and a constitutional monarchy acting through a locally-based Crown Commissioner would be minimal. It has to be recognised, nevertheless, that the choice between them would be seen by many as having a much greater symbolic importance. It is proposed, therefore, that within the referendum which would be needed in order to ratify a draft Welsh Constitution, electors be given the choice of supporting either a republic or a monarchy.

The legislature

It is proposed that the members of Wales's legislature, Senedd Cymru, should be elected by the Single Transferable Vote method of proportional representation, involving multi-member constituencies. The boundaries of these constituencies (which need not all have the same number of members since their populations would vary) should be determined by a Welsh

Electoral Commission following a process of consultation. The members of the Senedd should total in the region of 100.

The Senedd should be elected for a term of five years and an early election should only be possible if the existing government loses a motion of confidence and no alternative government, commanding the confidence of the Senedd, can be formed.

Although the Senedd should be the sole body with the power to make laws, there should also be a smaller, consultative, chamber – similar to the Slovene *Državni Svet* (National Council). Its membership should be nominated by social, economic, professional and local groups. All legislation should be referred to it before being finally enacted and it should have the power to require the Senedd to give further consideration to the proposed legislation in the light of the Council's views. It should also be able to put forward for consideration by the Senedd definite proposals for legislation either on its own initiative or in response to public petitions (see 'Citizen Initiative' below). In view of the novel nature of this proposal, its details, including its composition and how its members would be nominated call for extensive study and consultation.

The Executive

The Head of the Executive – the First Minister – should be appointed by the Head of State on the nomination of the Senedd. Other Ministers should be appointed by the Head of State on the nomination of the First Minister.

Ministers should be answerable to the Senedd but it is proposed that (other than the First Minister) they need not all be members of the Senedd. There is already a limited exception to the requirement that members of the Welsh Government be elected Members of the Senedd in that a person who is not a Member may be appointed Counsel General. The Counsel General, if not an MS, can take part in Senedd proceedings (but cannot vote). This mechanism, which enables a wider choice of appointee to be achieved in the case of a post requiring specialist legal knowledge, should be extended to enable Ministers holding other portfolios to be appointed from a wider group than elected Members.

The Welsh Government should be supported by an independent Welsh public service with constitutional status and independent institutions (such as a Welsh Public Service Commission) protecting its integrity and objectivity. The ability of Ministers to appoint temporary special advisers should be retained.

Regional/local government

Sub-national government, with a sound financial basis and powers to make local legislation in defined areas (similar to local byelaws but with wider scope) should be entrenched in the Constitution. The higher tier should be based on seven or eight historic, cultural, social and economic regions of Wales. The lower tier should be genuinely local, following a reorganisation of the current community and town level of local government, with their numbers reduced from the current 800 to around 300. This reorganisation should be undertaken by a Local Government Commission appointed for the purpose, whose terms of reference should include a requirement to undertake a process of consultation.

'Integrity' branch of government

The Constitution should recognise the importance of the developing 'integrity' branch of government, including Commissioners, Ombudsmen, Auditors and administrative tribunals, whose role is to scrutinise and improve the functioning of the Executive and other public bodies, in a similar way to that in which dedicated institutions in civil law systems operate, for example the French *Conseil d'Etat*. Appointments to these offices should be made by the Head of State with the agreement of the Senedd.

The judiciary

There should be an independent professional judiciary whose members are appointed by the Head of State on the recommendation of an independent Judicial Appointments Commission.

The courts should be organised into criminal, civil and family branches (with the ability to allocate cases to specialist chambers such as commercial and chancery courts), with a Welsh Court of Appeal. There should also be a Welsh Supreme Court whose function would be to rule on questions of the interpretation of the constitution (including whether legislation passed by the Parliament complied with the Constitution) as well as on general questions of Welsh law of particular difficulty or importance.

The Welsh Supreme Court should have the power to co-opt suitably-qualified eminent legal experts on to panels considering particularly important or difficult legal questions to which their expertise relates, not only when exercising the Court's constitutional jurisdiction but in relation to other cases where necessary.

Citizen initiative

Individual citizens should have the right to petition the National Council (that is, the consultative chamber forming part of the legislature) in favour of a specific legislative (including constitutional) change. The National Council should have the power, whether on the basis of such a petition or on its own initiative, to prepare a detailed case, including specific proposals for legislative reforms and to require the Welsh Government to give formal consideration to those proposals and to respond to them in detail, setting out how they intend to give effect to them or justifying their decision not to implement them.

Adopting and amending the Constitution

The Constitution would, once agreed by the Senedd by a two-thirds majority, need to be ratified by referendum. In the same way, any proposed amendment to the Constitution should require either:

i) a two-thirds majority in the Senedd; or

ii) if only approved by a simple majority in the Senedd, ratification by a simple majority in a referendum.

Recommendations

1. The path to an independent Wales with its own constitution should be a constitutional one. It should be achieved by a series of steps, the legality of which should be clear, and the provisions of which would therefore be recognised and enforced by public servants, including the judiciary, not only within Wales but in other jurisdictions.

2. Basic principles of a Welsh Constitution (to be defined in the Bill of Rights) should include:

    *   Democracy.
    *   Subsidiarity – that is, the principle that actions by the state can only be justified in order to achieve desirable social outcomes that cannot be achieved as effectively by individual efforts, and that such actions should always be taken at the most local level compatible with the effective achievement of the outcomes in question.
    *   The Rule of Law.
    *   Equality of all people.

- Individual and collective freedom
- Sustainability – that is, the principle that the needs of the present are to be met without harming the well-being of future generations by compromising the ability of those generations to meet their own needs.

3. Other characteristics of a Welsh Constitution should include:

- A declaration that Welsh sovereignty rests with the people of Wales.
- That it should include a description and role of Welsh governing institutions as well as the rights and responsibilities of citizens.
- That those rights and responsibilities should extend beyond the purely political and legalistic to encompass social and economic rights and responsibilities.
- That it should draw on best practice from around the world, especially constitutions that have been drawn up for small nations in analogous positions to that of Wales.

4. The Elements of a Welsh Constitution, as recommended by the Commission, represent an outline of the kind of Wales that could be achieved once Wales is independent.

5. The precise details of a Welsh Constitution will need to be discussed and agreed by the people of Wales and their representatives. This will be necessary to achieve the level of consensus and certainty which are essential if a constitution is to fulfil its purpose as the basic law of the state.

CHAPTER 9

A Welsh Self-Determination Bill

THIS CHAPTER MAKES RECOMMENDATIONS regarding a Welsh Self-Determination Bill that an incoming Plaid Cymru Government would promote in 2021. The Bill would cover:

1. The creation of a standing National Commission, with a full-time secretariat, to oversee the process leading to a referendum.
2. How to create Citizens' Assemblies to inform Welsh citizens on issues raised by independence.
3. How to hold polls and referenda to inform the Commission and the Welsh Government on public opinion regarding the issues of Welsh Self-Determination.

This chapter also considers and makes recommendations as to whether a referendum should be binary between the status quo and independence or provide for a multi-option choice.

Options for a Plaid Cymru Government

There are a number of ways in which the three objectives in the Bill might be delivered by an incoming Welsh Government in May 2021. Some, but not all, involve legislating. Each has advantages, disadvantages and difficulties, but there are also ways in which those can be overcome. There are broadly three options.

Option 1 – Primary Legislation

The advantages of this method include:

- Welsh Governments would be legally obligated to create and maintain a National Commission unless and until the Act requiring them to do so was repealed, which repeal would require a majority in the Senedd.
- The Commission could be established as a body independent of the Welsh Government, with the Welsh Government being duty bound to have regard to its recommendations.
- The Commission could be required to report to, and made answerable to, the Senedd rather than the Welsh Government.

Disadvantages and difficulties include:

- The legal difficulty: It is not within the legislative competence of the Senedd to enact provisions which relate to the "union of the nations of Wales and England".[89] Although it is not necessarily the case that the proposed legislation would (depending on its precise form) trespass on the reservation in question, there can be little doubt that the UK government would seek to characterise it as such and to challenge its validity in the Supreme Court.
- A political difficulty: To proceed by legislation would require that the Welsh Government have a working majority in the Senedd. Without such a majority, the support of at least one other party for the bill would be necessary to ensure its safe passage

Option 2 – A Bill to enable the Welsh Government to establish a National Commission

This method would involve passing an Act giving the Welsh Government the powers needed to establish the National Commission, the detailed operation of which would then be set out in subordinate legislation made by the Welsh Ministers. It would need to be decided how much detail about the Commission should be included on the face of the enabling Act and how much to leave to subordinate legislation. The choices made would need to be justified before the relevant Senedd committees scrutinising the bill. In addition, the Commission could be empowered to establish Citizens' Assemblies and conduct polls and referenda.

The advantages of this method include:

- The provisions in the parent Act could still place obligations upon the Welsh Government regarding the creation and maintenance of the Commission.
- The risk of challenges to legislation proving disruptive would be significantly reduced. Whereas a challenge to the provisions of a Bill or an Act could seriously delay setting up the Commission, or disrupt its working, a successful challenge to provisions in a statutory instrument could be remedied far more quickly.
- The Senedd would still be able to control the content of the subordinate legislation by requiring its making to be subject to an affirmative or even a super-affirmative resolution procedure, but would not be able to amend the content of that legislation during scrutiny.

The same legal and political difficulties as in Option 1 would apply to enacting and making the necessary legislation by this method. In addition:

- The Commission would be far less independent of the Welsh Government.
- The risk of a future government undermining or reversing the policy would be increased.
- The Senedd's control over the working of the Commission would decrease, although the Act could still require that the Commission report to the Senedd and that the

Welsh Government have due regard to Commission recommendations.

Option 3 – Welsh Government sets up a Convention without using legislation

This method would involve the Welsh Government establishing the National Commission or a Convention in the same manner as the Thomas Commission was established by the First Minister and the Silk Commission by the Secretary of State for Wales.

The advantages of this method include:

- It avoids the risk of challenge to legislative proposals or enactments on the grounds of competence, provided the Welsh Ministers use their executive powers in accordance with delegations made by the relevant parent Act. Ministers have no power to do things which would be outside the legislative competence of the Senedd.
- It avoids the political difficulties that would arise if the Government did not have a working majority in the Senedd.
- Since it gives control to the government as regards the operation of the Commission and Citizens' Assemblies reporting to it, there would be greater flexibility to adapt the operation of these bodies in the light of experience.

The disadvantages include:

- Loss of the independence that could be built into the constitution of a statutory body. In practice, previous Commissions and Conventions have enjoyed freedom from executive interference, but such self-denying abstinence cannot be validly equated with statutory independence.
- Limited, if any, role for the Senedd, other than what the Welsh Government chooses to give it.
- No guarantee that a future Welsh Government of a

different political complexion might not undermine or even terminate the arrangements, or simply ignore the Commission's recommendations.

- A lessening of the weight likely to be given to the views of the Commission and Assemblies – the more discretionary and consultative their nature is perceived to be (for example, because they are seen as not having a firm statutory basis) the less authoritative their deliberations may be felt to be.

Content of primary legislation

If a route involving primary legislation is chosen, the Bill should be drafted to include a purpose clause, which should aim to establish that neither the Bill nor any of its provisions relate to the union of the nations of Wales and England.

A useful precedent may be the wording used by the First Minister to establish the Commission on Justice in Wales (the previously mentioned Thomas Commission). This was established "to review the operation of the justice system in Wales and set a long-term vision for its future". This was done despite the fact that the Single Legal Jurisdiction of England and Wales is, like the union, a general reservation,[90] with the presence of a significant number of specific reservations concerning Justice listed under Part 2 of Schedule 7A. The purpose of the Bill might therefore be drafted to read something like "to obligate the Welsh Ministers to keep under review the operation of the institutions of devolved government in Wales and set a long term vision for their future".

If Option 1 is chosen, the Bill should have separate parts dealing with the National Commission, Citizens' Assemblies, and Referenda. Each part should be carefully related to the purpose provision. The Bill should have an Overview clause, distinct from its purpose clause, which introduces the role of the Commission, the Assemblies and the referenda as means of informing the Welsh Ministers regarding the operation of the devolved institutions and assisting them in forming a long term vision of their future.

The National Commission

This part of the Bill should make provision regarding issues such as the following:

- The remit of the Commission.
- The membership of the Commission – size, and geographical, functional and political representation.
- Commission staff.
- Powers and funding of the Commission.
- Location of secretariat.
- Reporting to the Senedd.

Citizens' Assemblies

This part of the Bill would, in addition to the same issues to be considered concerning the National Commission, need to make provision for the number and geographical distribution of the Citizens' Assemblies. Our recommendation however is that, regardless of whether Option 1 or Option 2 is chosen, the Bill should limit itself to enabling the Commission to establish the Assembly or Assemblies, thereby emphasising their independence of government.

The referendum

This is the most difficult element of the proposal to accommodate within the Senedd's legislative competence. A referendum involving the question of whether Wales should be an independent, sovereign state clearly relates to the union of Wales and England. Any legislation aiming to hold such a referendum is therefore outside the competence of the Senedd to enact. Therefore, on a wide, general interpretation of 'relating to the union', a referendum involving questions concerning different approaches to self-determination might also fall outside its powers.

Nevertheless, as with the other two goals, it should be possible to achieve the goal while avoiding issues of competence. Power could be given to the National Commission to hold polls or referenda to ascertain the opinion of the electorate on issues within its remit. The Bill, or subordinate legislation made by the Welsh Government under it, would need to set out:

- Who would be entitled to vote in such in such polls.
- How they were to be conducted.
- Provision with regard to incorporation of provisions from other enactments relating to polls and referenda.

The National Commission would then be able to report to the Government and make recommendations as to next steps. This would allow the Welsh Ministers to use their powers to take matters forward, for instance by making appropriate representations about the matters affecting Wales. The prohibition on the Welsh Ministers holding polls regarding whether and how that function should be exercised would not apply as it would not be the Welsh Ministers who had held the poll.

The results of such polls, and the recommendations made by the Commission in consequence, might be matters to which the Government was obligated to have regard.

It might be interesting to see whether 'the appropriate Minister' would consent to having a similar duty to have regard to such recommendations imposed upon the Secretary of State.[91]

Binary or multi-option choices in a referendum

This should be advised upon by the Commission and the Citizens' Assemblies rather than be provided for in legislation establishing those bodies. Leaving such issues to those bodies would also avoid difficulties concerning the competence of the Senedd to legislate regarding them.

Multi-option choices have been offered to electorates in other countries regarding constitutional issues. In New Zealand, for example, in the early 1990s, such an approach was taken regarding the proposal to change the electoral system. Two referenda were held. In the first, the voters were asked two questions:

1. Did they wish to move to a system of proportional representation?
2. If a majority did so wish, which system, from a range of options offered, would they wish to adopt?

A majority voted in favour of the change and selected a preferred system. The Government then produced the legislation necessary to effect the change, and submitted it to a further referendum, in effect telling the electorate that this was what the change entailed and asking them whether they still wished it to be done.

There is much to commend in this method, which combines an initial multi-choice approach with a final binary question, the detailed consequences of each choice being ascertainable before the final vote. This was the case with the March 2011 referendum in Wales on moving from the devolution settlement contained in Part 3 and Schedule 5 of the Government of Wales Act 2006 to that in Part 4 and Schedule 7.

An initial, multi-choice poll on the future form of Welsh self-determination could be conducted by the National Commission. However, any final binary choice – especially one involving an option of independence – would require further legislation in the form of an Order in Council under section 109(1) of the Government of Wales Act 2006, transferring the necessary legislative competence to the Senedd for this choice to be of binding effect.[92]

Practicalities of drafting the Bill

The Commission's Terms of Reference referred to a Welsh Self-Determination Bill as "paving legislation that an incoming Plaid Cymru Government will present to the Welsh civil service in 2021".

Legislative drafters regularly emphasise that they do not wish to receive instructions in the form of a draft. This is because they would have to assume that the draft correctly reflected the changes to the law that were required to deliver the underlying policy goals. Such an assumption is dangerous. What drafters, and the lawyers with whom they work, need to receive are clear, properly thought-through, policy instructions.

In terms of the proposed Self-Determination Bill, therefore, what needs to be ready by May 2021 are such policy instructions in relation to the proposed National Commission, Citizens' Assemblies and Referenda. Almost certainly, these instructions will raise further questions in what will become an iterative process of policy development leading to a final statement of the policy instructions.

Officials in the civil service working for the Welsh Government will almost certainly and rightly wish to rework those instructions to check that they are properly thought through before forwarding them, in the usual manner, to government lawyers who will then analyse them to determine what changes to the law are required to deliver the policy. They then, in turn, will forward legal instructions to the Office of Legislative Counsel, on the basis of which its drafters will prepare the Bill. The Bill will be prepared bilingually.

During the entire process, there will be regular communication between drafting counsel, the lawyers and policy officials, and also with Ministers when decisions need to be taken.

The question of whether a Self-Determination Bill can be

introduced early in the next Welsh Parliament will depend upon two key factors:

1. The relative importance attached to it as against the achievement of other policies requiring legislation for their delivery.
2. The readiness of the various policy projects in terms of detailed policy and legal instructions to enable bills to be drafted.

Even if it is decided to proceed by enacting legislation allowing the Welsh Government to establish a National Commission, the Senedd and its committees will almost certainly wish to know the detail of how that is to be done, and may well ask to see, as part of their scrutiny of the bill's proposals, a draft of the kind of regulations it is proposed to make.

Depending upon the priority placed upon the bill by the Government and the thoroughness of the policy presented to officials, the Bill could be ready for introduction by the autumn of 2021.

Recommendations

1. The setting up of a statutory National Commission to include the holding Citizens' Assemblies to inform the people of Wales about options for their constitutional future should be a key commitment in Plaid Cymru's Manifesto for the 2021 Senedd election.

2. Legislation under Option 2 – a Bill to establish the Commission with a broad remit, leaving it to subordinate legislation to settle the detail – is recommended as the best way forward. This would limit the disruptive effects of potential challenges on the grounds of competence, while preserving a measure of independence for the Commission and a meaningful role for the Senedd. An outline structure for such a draft bill is set out in Appendix 1.

3. The Bill should be drafted to include a purpose clause, making it clear that neither the Bill nor any of its provisions relate to the union of the nations of Wales and England.

4. It should be the Commission rather than Ministers in the Government that is authorised in the legislation to undertake a plebiscite on the future governance options for Wales.

5. The Commission should explore the New Zealand approach to testing the views of the people of Wales in an initial exploratory referendum, setting out constitutional options. It should be made clear that the outcome will be used to persuade the UK Westminster Government to agree to a binary referendum on the status quo versus the preferred choice in the first referendum.

CHAPTER 10

Bringing Wales with us

O UR REPORT WAS COMMISSIONED by Plaid Cymru and the party will have its own political messages to communicate in the run-up to the Senedd elections. But there are generic, value-based messages for all the people of Wales, who believe that gaining our independence is the best way to ensure a better, fairer, and happier future. As Adam Price says:

> "Creating a new Wales is not the work of one party, it is the work of an entire nation, all of its people and all of its perspectives."[93]

What follows is a summary of the principles that a Plaid Government and the statutory National Commission we recommend it should establish should follow in communicating the benefits of independence.

Building national self-confidence

Consistently telling or implying that people (or nations) are too small or insignificant, too poor or too dependent to stand on their own two feet leads to a self-fulfilling prophecy. Large swathes of the people of Wales believe this myth and have questioned our ability to survive alone.

But it is not true. Wales is not too small, too poor and can wash its own face. As we have shown in Chapter 5 of this report, Wales currently has an economic deficit in common with the whole of the United Kingdom apart from London and the English south-east. We are held back by this longstanding imbalance which is a consequence of an overweening concentration of political power and investment in just one part of England. Independence offers Wales the chance to create a different future. It is the case that Ireland, for example, would not have achieved so much economically if it had remained a part of the United Kingdom.

If you don't believe this, it is still worth giving the idea that we can stand on our own feet the benefit of the doubt. Start by questioning the 'common wisdom' of Unionists, that has until now been accepted as 'the truth'. There's no rush – we are not going to be seeking independence tomorrow. We understand that many people are Indy-curious, that is to say, they are open-minded and want to know more.

We are confident that our report provides many of the answers and will assist our national self-confidence to grow so that we no longer feel unable to govern ourselves.

Currently, Plaid Cymru is the only party that offers to deliver an independent Wales. However, it is not an exclusive project. As our survey in Chapter 2 reveals, there is growing support for independence across parties, and especially within the Labour Party.

Sustainability

Sustainability and well-being of future generations are core Welsh values that must be central to an independent Wales, whatever the political alignment that ensures it happens.

The Government of Wales Act 2006 places the promotion of sustainable development at the heart of Senedd Cymru's work. Wales remains one of the few administrations in the world to have such a statutory duty. It is an opportunity to develop Wales as a small, smart nation, in ways that will contribute sustainably to people's economic, social and environmental wellbeing.

The 2007 One Wales Coalition Government's Sustainable Development Scheme, 'One Wales One Planet', laid the foundation for the subsequent Well-being of Future Generations Act in 2015. The process of developing the Act was inclusive. It had cross-party support and many individuals and organisations contributed to the national discussion on 'the Wales we want'. It is appropriate, therefore, to consider independence through the lens of this progressive act and to use it as a framework to develop our approach to independence.

The overarching ambition of any Welsh Government led by Plaid Cymru will be to ensure that we can meet our needs (not our greeds) and create a future that our children and grandchildren will be proud of. We will do this without over-exploiting the natural environment and ensure that we can prosper in a globally responsible way as a member of the family of nations.

The four pillars of an independent Wales

A Plaid Cymru Government should develop a programme that gives equal priority to the **economy**, our **people**, the **environment**, and our **culture**. It isn't good enough to think of these individually – a table needs four sturdy legs of equal length, not one or two longer or shorter than the other.

We want a strong economy but not a dog-eat-dog one – where some people have too much, and others don't have enough. We want to live in a fair Wales where people are valued for who they are not for how much money they have. Those are our values. We have a beautiful country full of natural resources that we can enjoy and manage in a low-carbon, sustainable way. And we have a language that's unique to Wales – a language for everyone.

Everyone should be given a chance to learn it. Having more than one language is like having more than one window in your house – it enables you to see, feel and experience many more things.

A five-point plan for success

1. Independence will be a slow burn process, where we work together to find out what's best for Wales. We need to establish how we can be a normal country looking after our own business, our own people, and how we should manage our own environment, while also enjoying our particular cultures and languages in our own way.

2. Every day, when we wake-up we have to make decisions. When Wales is in a position to make decisions regarding its own destiny, the very least we will insist on is that all decisions '**do no harm**'. We don't want things getting any worse for the people of Wales. Normal countries make things better for their citizens, and that is what we shall strive for in an independent Wales.

3. It is easy to get fed up when things aren't **joined up**. An independent Wales will do things better than the status quo. Our Welsh NHS is a great example. We've already seen that a devolved Wales and Scotland have been able to deal with the Covid-19 crisis in a much more effective local way, putting the focus on keeping us safe. Just imagine what an independent Wales could achieve – a cradle to grave, seamless system putting people, not profit, first. There is absolutely nothing stopping us from achieving this, except that we are trapped in a system that we currently don't fully control.

4. **Doing things together** as families and communities is the Welsh way – there are amazing stories of how we pulled together during the Covid-19 crisis. When we become a normal country, looking after our own affairs, we can focus

on nurturing our small local businesses and promoting our own produce For example, in Norway supermarkets don't stock mass-produced bread in plastic bags. Everyone buys their fresh bread from their local baker. We will be looking to small nations for other examples of best practice so we can grow Wales into a more prosperous nation.

5. **Bringing everyone with us** will be such an exciting national project. Anyone who wants to be Welsh is Welsh and must feel they belong. Wales is a country that is tolerant and embraces difference. We need to let the world know that this is what characterises our nation.

The independent Wales we want

A prosperous Wales: That means a Wales in control of its own economy, promoting innovation in low-carbon, clean industries. We will be using **our** resources efficiently and taking climate change seriously. We can make sure that our people are skilled and well-educated. Our economy will generate wealth for us, there will be satisfying, decent, fairly-paid jobs.

A resilient Wales: *Yma o hyd* ('Still here'), our famous alternative national anthem, captures the spirit of our resilience. With the freedom to 'do our own thing' we can plan to make sure that our biodiverse natural environment is maintained and enhanced – not just seen as a theme park for city dwellers to admire at weekends (and who can blame them) but as our home, the place where people live and work. We will have healthy functioning ecosystems that support social, economic and ecological resilience coupled with the capacity to adapt to change. We'll be ready to face whatever the post-Covid 19 world, Brexit and climate change have to throw at us.

 A healthier Wales: The overall health of many people in Wales is not as good as it should be. Things can be different in an independent Wales. Improving the economy and having a focus on low carbon, clean industries will be a start. We can help people help themselves to improve their physical and mental well-being and make sensible choices for themselves and their families.

 A more equal Wales: The Black Lives Matter movement has shone a light on inequality which currently is the norm. When Wales becomes independent, we will have the opportunity to ensure everyone can fulfil their potential. We will be able to identify the structures and barriers that are preventing this from happening and take steps to dismantle them, one by one.

 A Wales of cohesive communities: Wales is already a patchwork of communities where people look out for each other. An independent Wales will ensure that these become even more attractive, viable, safe and well-connected.

 A Wales with a vibrant culture and thriving Welsh language: The Welsh language is a national treasure whether you currently speak it or not. It should be accessible to everyone, and we should ensure the barriers to learning are removed. An independent Wales will promote and protect our culture, heritage and the Welsh language. It will also encourage the people of Wales to participate in the arts, sports and recreation.

 A globally responsible Wales: Our aim is to improve our economic, social, environmental and cultural well-being. We will do so in a way that makes a positive contribution to the rest of the world. An independent Wales will be known as a friendly country whose people others will want to do business with because they respect us and what we stand for.

These values transcend party politics. They are framed within the 2015 Well-being of Future Generations Act, which captures the spirit and essence of two decades of United Nations work in the area of sustainable development and serves as a model for other regions and countries. In his visit to Wales in 2015 Nikhil Seth, former Head of Sustainable Development at the United Nations, said:

> "We hope that what Wales is doing today the world will do tomorrow. Action, more than words, is the hope for our current and future generations."

Creating an independent Wales will be an inspiring journey. As Adam Price says, our vision is being led by Plaid Cymru, but it is one for the whole nation.

Outline Content of a Welsh Self-Determination Bill

WHAT FOLLOWS IS A very simple outline draft of the kind of provisions that would be needed to deliver a Bill in accordance with Option 2 in Chapter 9. It is not intended to be, nor is it, a draft bill.

It leaves open the question of how much detail concerning the membership and operation of the Commission should appear on the face of the Bill and how much should be left to subordinate legislation ('the Regulations'). If greater detail regarding the Commission's membership and operation were to appear on the face of the Bill, these would probably be placed in a Schedule or Schedules at its end, and sections 7 and 8 would make reference to the Schedule(s).

By convention, the short title of a bill is settled by drafting counsel and is not the subject of political choice.

Self-Determination (Wales) Bill

[OUTLINE ONLY]

An Act to place a duty upon the Welsh Ministers to keep the operation of the institutions of government in Wales under review and set a long term vision for their future; to establish a National Commission to assist them in discharging that duty and make provision for its functions ; and for connected purposes.

Introductory

1. Purpose of the Act

This Act:

(a) imposes a duty upon Welsh Ministers to keep the operation of the institutions of government in Wales under review and set a long-term vision for their future;

(b) makes provision for the creation of a National Commission to assist the Welsh Ministers in the discharge of that duty, together with the functions of the Commission;

(c) makes provision regarding the relation of the National Commission to the Welsh Ministers and other bodies.

Duties of the Welsh Ministers

2. To keep the operation of the institutions of government of Wales under review

The Welsh Ministers must keep the operation of the institutions of government in Wales under review and set a long-term vision for their future.

3. To establish a National Commission

(1) The Welsh Minsters must, within x months of the coming into force of this Act, establish a National Commission to advise them and make recommendations to them concerning the discharge of their duty under section 2.

(2) The Welsh Ministers must establish the National Commission by regulations ("the regulations").

(3) In making the regulations, the Welsh Ministers must have due regard to the need for diversity within the membership of the Commission in order to achieve geographical, functional, political, racial, linguistic, age and gender representation.

(4) The Welsh Ministers must make provision for a secretariat to serve the National Commission.

4. Power to amend the regulations

(1) The Welsh Ministers may amend the regulations from time to time.

(2) Amendments to the regulations must be made by further regulations.

(3) Amendments to the regulations may include amendments to the Commission's terms of reference and functions.

(4) Amendments to the regulations may be made by way of addition, modification or removal.

5. Duty of the Welsh Ministers to have due regard to the Commission's recommendations

The Welsh Ministers must have due regard to recommendations made by the Commission.

6. Duty of the Welsh Ministers to report to the Senedd

The Welsh Ministers must report annually to the Senedd regarding their responses to advice received from and recommendations made by the Commission, and the actions they have taken.

The National Commission

7. Terms of Reference

The regulations made by the Welsh Ministers must provide terms of reference for the National Commission.

8. Membership

(a) The regulations must make provision for the membership of the National Commission, including:

(b) the number of its members;

(c) the manner of their appointment;

(d) the qualifications for appointment, including any disqualifications;

(e) the length of time that members may serve;

(f) the eligibility or otherwise of members for re-appointment;

(g) reasons for which a member's membership may be suspended or terminated, including procedures for suspension and termination;

(h) any entitlement of members to remuneration, reimbursement of expenses or other payments.

9. Duty of the Commission to inform itself of Welsh public opinion

(1) In the discharge of its duty to advise the Welsh Ministers, the Commission must take steps to inform itself of the opinion of the public in Wales regarding the operation of the institutions of government in Wales.

(2) In order to inform itself of public opinion in Wales, the Commission may:

(a) establish one or more Citizens' Assemblies;

(b) conduct polls and referenda.

(3) In establishing Citizens' Assemblies, the Commission must have due regard to the need for diversity in order to achieve geographical, functional, political, racial, linguistic, age and gender representation within their membership.

(4) The Welsh Ministers must make such provision as is necessary to enable the Commission to establish Citizens' Assemblies and conduct polls and referenda where the Commission has decided to do so.

10. Duty of the Commission to Report to the Senedd

(1) The Commission must report annually to the Senedd on its work.

(2) The Commission's annual report must include reports on:

(a) the advice it has given to the Welsh Ministers;

(b) the recommendations it has made to the Welsh Ministers;

(c) the advice or recommendations it has received from Citizens' Assemblies;

(d) the conduct and results of polls or referenda it has conducted.

11. Power of the Commission to make other recommendations

The Commission may also make recommendations regarding the operation and future of the institutions of government in Wales to:

(a) the Senedd;

(b) the Secretary of State.

Duty of the Secretary of State

12. Secretary of State to have due regard to the Commission's recommendations

In discharging the functions of his office, the Secretary of State must have due regard to recommendations of the Commission.

Miscellaneous Provisions

13. Regulations

(1) Powers to make regulations under this Act must be exercised by statutory instrument.

(2) Regulations may not be made unless a draft of the instrument has been laid before, and approved by a resolution of, the Senedd.

14. Coming into force and Short title

(1) This Act shall come into force upon receiving Royal Assent.

(2) This Act may be cited as The Self-Determination (Wales) Act 2022.

Independence Commission

Terms of Reference

The Independence Commission will undertake analysis, develop possible policy options, and prepare pathways to independence for an incoming Plaid Cymru government in 2021.

The starting point for the Commission's agenda will be the paper 'Wales 2030: Seven Steps to Independence', published by Adam Price during his leadership campaign in August 2018. However, the group will operate at arms-length from the party's mainstream policy-making processes. This is a deliberate effort to engage wider Welsh civil society in the debate around independence. As 'Seven Steps to Independence' declared:

"Creating a new Wales is not the work of one party, it is the work of an entire nation, all of its people and all of its perspectives."

'Seven Steps to Independence' proposed the creation of a standing National Commission whose work will enable the people of Wales to make an informed choice in the referendum that is envisaged to take place by 2030. The Independence Commission is seen as a forerunner of this National Commission.

The Commission will need to give special attention to the European dimension and developments around Brexit, given the present uncertainties. Its work will need to be tailored to the range of potential scenarios that are likely to emerge during the coming year.

There will be five inter-related strands to the Independence Commission's agenda:

1. The economic case: closing the fiscal gap

The Welsh fiscal gap – the difference between income from taxes raised in Wales and expenditure on public services, welfare payments and pensions – has been used to argue that an independent Wales simply couldn't pay its way. It is important to turn this argument on its head, and there are signs that this is beginning to happen in contemporary public discourse in Wales: we are relatively poor (within the UK) because we are not independent.

Of course, an independent Wales should not be under an obligation to balance its books, as most advanced countries run a fiscal deficit. However, this needs to be at a level that is sustainable so that there will be no disruption to public services or welfare payments and pensions. The Commission will undertake an analysis and produce recommendations on policies an incoming Plaid Cymru government should pursue over a ten-year period to ensure that the Welsh fiscal gap is reduced to bring it within, say, six per cent of the UK average.

2. Establishing a distinctive Welsh jurisdiction and justice system

A distinctive jurisdiction encompasses a defined territory, a body of law, a separate structure of courts and separate legal institutions. Scotland and Northern Ireland comprise distinctive jurisdictions in this sense. Yet, notwithstanding having a defined territory and developing its own body of law since the onset of legislative devolution, Wales remains combined with England in a single jurisdiction. This is despite the 2006 and 2014 Wales Acts which established the Assembly's competence to make primary legislation, and the 2017 Wales Act which changed the system for determining the powers of the Assembly from a 'conferred powers' to a 'reserved powers' model. Taking into account the work of the Commission on Justice in Wales, chaired by Lord Thomas of Cwmgiedd, that reported in November 2019, the Independence Commission will recommend ways that a distinctive Welsh jurisdiction and justice system can be progressed

3. A Welsh Constitution

The Commission will draw up a Written Constitution for an independent Wales. The starting point will be a declaration that Welsh sovereignty rests with the people of Wales. The Constitution should include a description of the place and role of Welsh governing institutions as well as the rights and responsibilities of citizens. The latter should extend beyond the purely political and legalistic to encompass social and economic rights and responsibilities. In drawing up the Written Constitution the Commission should draw on best practice from around the world, especially constitutions that have been drawn up for small nations in analogous positions to that of Wales. For example, there has been a process in Scotland that is worthy of examination.

The Commission should aim to present a draft Constitution to a specially convened Citizens' Assembly in the early part of 2020 before finalising its recommendations.

4. Relations of an independent Wales with the rest of the UK, and the European Union

An independent Wales would still need and wish to maintain close economic, social and cultural ties with the rest of the UK, Ireland and the European Union, but on the basis of a new pattern of relationships. Taking into account Adam Price's speech on 'Benelux Britain', to the Centre of Constitutional Change at Edinburgh University in June 2019, the Commission will explore the options available and provide recommendations. Specifically, these will examine the constitutional relationships between the Benelux countries and the extent to which they might be applied within the British Isles.

In addition, this part of the Commission's work will need to address:

1. The desirability of maintaining a frictionless border between an independent Wales and England.
2. The defence and security profile that an independent Wales would adopt.

5. A Welsh Self-Determination Bill

This will be paving legislation that an incoming Plaid Cymru Government will present to the Welsh civil service in 2021. It is referred to as a 'Self-Determination' rather than 'Independence' Bill since it would be designed to engage with as wide a cross-party consensus as possible. Included in the Bill will be:

1. The creation of a standing National Commission, with a full-time secretariat, to oversee the process leading to a referendum.
2. A process of Citizen's Assemblies to inform Welsh citizens on issues raised by independence
3. Consideration of whether referendum should be binary

between the status quo and independence or provide for a multi-option choice.

6. Time frame

The Commission should hold its first meeting before the end of 2019 and publish its findings during September 2020.

Commissioners' biographies

Elfyn Llwyd (Chair of the Independence Commission) is a barrister and was Plaid Cymru MP for Meirionnydd Nant Conwy from 1992 to 2010 and for Dwyfor Meirionnydd from 2010 to 2015. In February 2019 he was appointed shadow counsel general for Plaid Cymru in the Senedd and sits as a member of the Shadow Cabinet. At Westminster he was the party's parliamentary group leader, becoming a member of the Privy Council in 2011. Born and brought up mainly in Betws-y-Coed, Elfyn was educated in Llanrwst and later attended the University of Wales, Aberystwyth and Chester Law College. He was a partner at Guthrie Jones and Jones, Solicitors in Dolgellau and Bala from 1978 to 1996 and President of the Gwynedd Law Society in 1990-91. He was called to the bar in 1997. In Parliament Elfyn was the first to initiate a Bill calling for the setting up of a Children's Commissioner for Wales in 1993. He amended the Family Law Act 1996 to enhance the voice and interests of children in divorce situations. In 2012 he introduced a private Bill to establish in the criminal law the offence of stalking which was accepted by Government and enacted. Similarly, his Bill to criminalise coercive control within domestic violence was introduced by him in February 2015 and was accepted by Government and became law in January 2016. He chaired the

All Party Justice Unions Group and the All Party Family Court Unions Group as well as serving as vice-chair of the Justice Select Committee in which role he chaired public and private sessions of the Committee and represented the Committee and Parliament in International Justice conferences. From 2011-2015 he was a Parliamentary Advisor to the Police Federation.

Carys Aaron has enjoyed a varied career, being a retired teacher, business manager, and law lecturer and tutor. Having studied English Literature at the University of Wales, Bangor in the 1970s, she followed the obvious path and became a teacher. At the same time, she and her husband embarked on a business venture, establishing the first precarious independent television company in north Wales in 1978, with Carys being responsible for all the contractual and financial matters. When family responsibilities arrived, she gave up teaching but continued to be involved with the incipient business. For over 25 years she continued in this role, ultimately responsible for nearly 100 permanent staff and over 500 freelancers, and an annual financial turnover of over £12million. Carys retired from the company in 2005 and started volunteering for the local Citizens' Advice Bureau. This kindled her interest in the law, which led to a law degree course (again at Bangor University), a first-class LLB, and the prestigious Sir Samuel Evans Memorial Prize for being the best law student in any Welsh university. She was appointed a tutor and part-time lecturer in law at Bangor University on her graduation. She concentrated on Constitutional Law and European Law, always with the Welsh context in mind. She very much enjoyed the teaching and the sometimes lively interaction with the students, yet feels that her greatest contribution as a law academic was facilitating the Coleg Cymraeg Cenedlaethol project to provide textbooks in the Welsh language for all law students at our universities. Carys is the company secretary of Galeri Caernarfon Cyf, a not-for-profit community enterprise. She is also a board member of Sistema Cymru – Codi'r To (a community regeneration project that brings the world-renowned El Sistema teaching method to north Wales) and of Crochan Celf (which aims to improve the conditions of life of those in need through the medium of arts). Carys has always had a political perspective. Her career has reinforced her belief that Wales as a nation cannot move forwards without our own independent jurisdiction.

Cynog Dafis was MP for Ceredigion from 1992 to 2000, and AM for the Senedd's Mid and West region from 1999 to 2003. He is a former editor of *Y Ddraig Goch* and Plaid Cymru director of publications. He was Director of Policy from 1998 to 2003. He was for many years active in Welsh-language campaigning, having been chair of Cymdeithas yr Iaith Gymraeg and author of its first Manifesto (1971) and a leading member of campaigns for Welsh-medium education in Dyfed. He has written extensively on bilingualism and Welsh Nationalism. He was until 2011 a founder board member of Cantref Housing Association, and one-time chair. He was a member of the executive and vice-chair of Tomorrow's Wales, the civil society movement which led the campaign for legislative powers for the National Assembly of Wales. He was a trustee of the Centre for Alternative Technology and President of the homelessness charity Ceredigion Care. He is a fellow of the Universities of Aberystwyth and Trinity Saint David's. His autobiography *Mab y Pregethwr* (The Preacher's Son) was published in November 2005. In 2016 he co-authored with Aled Jones Williams the volume *Duw yw'r Broblem* (God is the Problem).

Rhys David was born in Cardiff and has an MA degree in Literae Humaniores from the University of Oxford. He began his career in journalism at the *Western Mail*, where he held the posts successively of Chief Leader Writer, Industrial Editor, and Welsh Affairs Editor. He subsequently spent 30 years at the *Financial Times*, holding senior writing posts dealing with UK and international business sectors. His posts included Northern Ireland correspondent in Belfast during the Troubles in the 1970s and he was later UK Northern Correspondent based in Manchester. Writing briefs in London included the international chemicals, pharmaceuticals, fibres, textiles, and clothing industries, aluminium and steel. Editing roles at the FT included responsibility for the 200 multi page reports published annually on countries, regions, business sectors, financial and management topics, personal finance, information technology and education. During his employment at the FT he also spent three years as managing director and publisher of *Business*, a magazine joint subsidiary of the FT and US publisher, Condé Nast, and was a BP press fellow at Wolfson College, Cambridge in 1986. On leaving the FT he worked as assistant director of the Institute of Welsh Affairs in Cardiff where he worked on numerous research reports on aspects of Welsh society and economy, as well as contributing numerous articles to the institute's journal, *Agenda*, and various other Welsh and UK media and journals. Major commissioned works which he co-authored alongside university partners during this period include 'The Socio-Economic Characteristics of the South Wales Valleys in a Broader Context', comparing and contrasting the recovery and performance of former coal and steel producing areas in Wales with other parts of the UK, and 'Auditing Welsh Industry, A Clusters based Approach', which looked at the interlinkages within different sectors, including Wales's aerospace industry. Other publications include *Roaring Dragons: Entrepreneurial Tales from Wales,* an examination of selected successful Welsh small businesses, and *Tell Mum not to Worry,* an account of the 53rd (Welsh) Division's campaigns in the Near East in World War One. He is a council member of the

Honourable Society of Cymmrodorion and has been a fellow of the Royal Society for the Arts since 1986.

Eurfyl ap Gwilym is Plaid Cymru's Economics Adviser and a former National Chair and Director of Research with the party. He was a non-executive director and deputy chair of the Principality Building Society for nine years and continues as chair of the Principality Pension Trustees. He has been a director of four companies that have listed on the London Stock Exchange during his tenure as a director. His early career was with Unilever, the John Williams Group, Philips and GE. When with GE he was a member of the CBI President's Council and was GE National Executive for the UK and Ireland. Eurfyl has served as a member or chair of a number of audit and remuneration committees including the audit committee of the National Museum of Wales. Eurfyl is a director and trustee of the Institute of Welsh Affairs and a member of the University of Wales Investment Committee and the Fiscal Advisory Board of Cardiff University's Wales Governance Centre. He is the author of numerous papers and articles in English and Welsh on constitutional, financial and economic matters and was a member of the UK Government's Commission on Devolution in Wales (the Silk Commission). Eurfyl has spoken at many international conferences, symposia and seminars on constitutional and fiscal matters. Eurfyl was born and brought up in Aberyswyth and from 1963 to 1969 he attended Kings College, London, where he obtained a BSc and Phd in Physics. He is a frequent contributor to BBC and S4C current affairs programmes. He is married to Siwan and has four children.

Dr Jonathan Huish was brought up in Pontyclun. With a background spanning economics, psychology and business leadership, he has held leadership roles at board and senior management levels, within public and private sector organisations across the world. Jonathan started his career in the financial sector, working with companies such as Standard Chartered and Goldman Sachs. He then made the move to the public sector, holding a range of leadership roles. Over the course of his career, Jonathan has worked with more than 70 major public organisations, including Welsh Government, to support and deliver transformational change and improvement. Jonathan is currently the Chair of Trivallis, one of Wales's largest social landlords, and Chief Executive of Capital People, a consultancy that provides training in organisational development, HR, strategy, leadership, governance, and health, safety and the environment. Previous roles have included Deputy Leader of Rhondda, Cynon Taf; Advisor to Belfast Council, the Northern Ireland Assembly, and the Governments of Singapore, Ghana, Kenya, and South Africa. He currently coaches a number of leaders, chief executives, chairs and ministers from across public and private sectors. Jonathan was recently appointed as a board member of Community Housing Cymru; was elected as the chair of the Chairs and Vice Chairs' Strategic Group of Housing Associations in Wales; and is a member of the newly established Housing Thought Leadership Group. He also chairs Artis, the largest of the ACW funded participative arts organisations, based in the Welsh Valleys.

Fflur Jones was brought up in Llanuwchllyn. After gaining degrees in History and Legal and Political Theory at Cambridge University and UCL respectively, she qualified as a solicitor in 2003 and joined Cardiff commercial law firm Darwin Gray. She became a partner in 2010 and head of its employment and human resources team in 2013. Fflur's employment law practice includes a particular expertise and interest in discrimination law. As well as being a regular contributor to radio and TV programmes, Fflur is an experienced trainer, having delivered courses on a wide range of employment law topics. She is a regular speaker at different functions and conferences on issues surrounding mental health in the workplace. Fflur was instrumental in establishing the Wales Human Resources Network in 2016. Every year the network hosts a variety of educational events for HR professionals, and also hosts the prestigious annual Wales HR Awards to celebrate the achievements of professionals across Wales. Fflur's other area of specialisms include Regulatory Compliance. She is extremely interested in legislative matters arising out of Devolution and Brexit. She has written papers on developing a separate jurisdiction for Wales and on the EU Withdrawal Bill and has participated in a conference in the European Parliament on the Reform of European Electoral Law. She has also given evidence to the Justice in Wales Commission. Recently she completed a review and report on the Welsh Government's Major Events Unit's strategy. Fflur is chair of Plaid Cymru's Discipline, Standards and Membership Committee, and chair of Menter a Busnes. She is also a board member of Aloud, and Sinfonia Cymru.

Glyndwr Cennydd Jones has been the chief executive officer of a UK-wide industry body since 2012, based in London, having previously held a senior role at an international awarding organisation for more than 11 years. His professional activities with education authorities, ministers and regulators has involved negotiating strategic targets which demand analysis, evaluation and synthesis of information and established practices from a wide range of sources. He stood as a Senedd and Parliamentary candidate for Plaid Cymru during the period of the party's One Wales coalition with Labour. Glyndwr is an advocate for greater cross-party consensus in Wales and for a UK-wide convention, and has been published on these themes by the *Western Mail*, Institute of Welsh Affairs, *Golwg*, *Y Cymro*, Cardiff University, and the Centre on Constitutional Change. He has also contributed to two booklets involving Elystan Morgan and David Owen. A catalogue of his articles and essays can be found on: https://constitutionalcontinuum.blogspot.com/

Menna Jones was brought up in Alltyblaca, Ceredigion, and works in the social enterprise sector in Gwynedd. She is a passionate advocate for community-based social business and co-operatives that can best meet the social, environmental, and health and well-being needs of communities in Wales. A graduate of Aberystwyth University she worked for Dr Carl Clowes, at Gwynedd Health Authority. Later she worked as Caernarfon constituency secretary for Dafydd Wigley MP when she adopted a strong work ethic, commitment to equality, social justice and community-led development. Joining Cymdeithas Tai Eryri, she managed social housing with annual development programmes of £5million and specialised in special needs projects, creating community management models focusing on homelessness, mental health issues, substance misuse and learning disability homes. After a short period developing after school and childcare projects across north Wales, she joined Antur Waunfawr. Over the last 24 years she has developed the organisation from a small charity employing ten staff to a vibrant social enterprise employing 110 staff and supporting 75 people with learning disabilities with a turnover of £3million. The company runs 14 projects, is administered in Welsh, and includes recycling/reuse, day services, well-being and environmental projects, supported housing and 24-hour care. She has been a board member of Menter a Busnes for the last ten years, is Vice-chair of Canolfan Iaith Nantgwrtheyrn, and has just become a board member of the Wales Co-operative Movement. A Big Ideas Wales role model visiting north Wales secondary schools, she has previously been a committee member of Galeri Cyf, Gisda Cyf, Cymdeithas Tai Hafan, Gwynedd Economic Committee, Arloesi (Leader), Women's Aid, Canolfan Bro

Llanwnda, and has strong links with social enterprise providers in Gwynedd and throughout Wales. Recently she became a Social Enterprise Academy facilitator (affiliated to SEA Scotland) and is an active member of Yes Caernarfon. She is intent on working with a range of communities, enterprises and grass roots organisations to understand and dissect the Welsh economy and re-align models to promote sustainability and support for self-determination and independence.

Elen ap Robert was born in Aberystwyth and brought up in Cardiff. She attained a first-class honours degree in music at Sheffield University before pursuing postgraduate vocal studies at the Guildhall School of Music and Drama, London. Elen then joined Glyndebourne Festival and Touring Opera Chorus, undertaking understudy and principal soprano roles and was nominated for the Christie Award during the summer season of Mozart operas in 1991. Her career as a professional singer spanned eight years and included performing the role of Juliet in the Thames Television/Channel 4 film adaptation of Benjamin Britten's opera *The Little Sweep* directed by Basil Coleman and performing new commissions by Welsh composers including Dilys Elwyn Edwards. She was awarded the Grace Williams Memorial Prize by Arts Council Wales in 1990 and in the same year became a founder member of the Welsh branch of the Yehudi Menuhin scheme for young performers, LIVE MUSIC NOW! Her experience as a performer on the scheme for seven years led her to develop an interest in the transformative effect of music on those who are disadvantaged and she went on to complete a postgraduate diploma in Music Therapy in 1997 at the Royal Welsh College of Music and Drama before spending five years working as a music therapist in north-west Wales. In 2004 Elen became arts development officer for Galeri Caernarfon Cyf, and on opening, became Galeri Creative Enterprise Centre's first Artistic

Director – a role she held until 2012. During her time at Galeri she developed the artistic direction of the centre, programming across the arts spectrum, forging key national creative partnerships and focussing on reaching audiences less likely to engage with the arts. In April 2012, Elen was appointed the first Artistic Director of Bangor University's flagship development, brand new Arts and Innovation Centre, Pontio, which, following a period of delay, finally opened its doors to the public in December 2015. Elen led on developing the artistic vision for the centre, creating its ambitious inaugural programme of events, and for the following four years has established an artistic offer with a particular emphasis on quality arts empowering the community, using accessible art forms such as circus, along with music and participatory theatre activities to connect with a broad spectrum of audiences and groups, including those not traditionally engaging with the arts. Elen has also led on the creation of unique arts/science and arts in health collaborations as well as the nurturing and supporting of artists and Welsh medium and bilingual theatre. In August 2019 she moved on from Pontio to become an arts consultant. Elen is board member of Welsh National Opera, is newly-appointed arts associate for Arts Council Wales, chairs the cultural subgroup of the National Eisteddfod and sits on the advisory group on Brexit for Welsh Government. She lives in Felinheli, is married and has three grown-up children.

Dr Einir Young was born in the Rhondda and brought up in Cwmtwrch in the Swansea Valley. She has a degree in Agriculture from Aberystwyth, a PGCE from Trinity College Carmarthen and a PhD from Bangor University. Following a brief interlude as a post-doctoral research fellow at the University of California, Davis, she returned to Bangor where, 24 years later, she is now the Director of Sustainability at Bangor University and leads the University's Sustainability Lab team. Her work focusses on embedding sustainability and well-being across institutions and communities. At Bangor University she has a remit to drive sustainability through all facets of the organisation adopting the Well-being of Future Generations (Wales 2015) Act as a tool for making sense of the complexity of Sustainability and a framework for action. She worked for many years on projects that addressed the impacts of climate change on the livelihoods of resource-poor communities in sub-Saharan Africa and the management and policy options required for sustainable development in the region. She notes that not once, in any of the African countries where she has worked – which include Benin, Botswana, Côte d'Ivoire, Eritrea, Ethiopia, Ghana, Kenya, Lesotho, Mali, Nigeria, Sierra Leone, South Africa, Uganda, and Zimbabwe – has anyone suggested that they would be better off forfeiting their independence to be ruled by their former colonial masters. Ghana is the country closest to her heart. In 1998 she was made a Queen Mother of Gomoa Obiri, a small village in the Cape Coast region and she has maintained close ties with the people there for more than 20 years. The new Prime Minister of Lesotho is a former collaborator and personal friend. She has since turned her focus to Wales, where the climate is less harsh but the challenges much the same – a global need for people everywhere to live well within the carrying capacity of the planet. Her most recent publication is 'The intangible made tangible in Wales', a chapter in *The Routledge Companion to Intangible Cultural Heritage*, which describes the value of cultural heritage and the importance of agility, flexibility and the ability to adapt and change to sustainable economic development. She is the chair and one of the founding members of RCE Cymru, the pan-Wales Regional Centre of Expertise for Sustainability, part of the UN Network of 174 such centres globally. She is a member of the Board of Academi Heddwch Cymru (Wales Peace Academy) and chairs Cyngor Gwynedd's Standards Committee. She lives in Talybont, Bangor, is married and has a dog. Her passion is walking long distance paths.

Legal Advice

The Commission has benefited from the advice and active engagement of two eminent Welsh lawyers with experience in legislation and government:

Keith Bush QC LLM (London) is a Fellow in Welsh Law in the Wales Governance Centre (having previously been an Honorary Professor of Law at Swansea University). He was, until August 2019, President of the Welsh Language Tribunal, and has served as a Recorder (sitting in the County Court), a member of the Law Commission's Advisory Committee for Wales, and Secretary of the Wales Public Law and Human Rights Association. He is currently Treasurer of the Legal Wales Foundation and Director of the annual Legal Wales Conference. Having practised at the bar in Cardiff for over 20 years, he joined the Welsh Government's legal service in 1999, where he became Legislative Counsel, leading the legal team which worked on a number of bills relating to Wales, including the one that became the Government of Wales Act 2006. From 2007 until 2012 he was Chief Legal Adviser to the National Assembly for Wales. He has contributed to the *Statute Law Review*, the *Cambrian Law Review*, the Wales Legal Journal, the Journal of the Welsh Legal History Society, the *New Law Journal* and the *Tribunals Journal*, and he frequently lectures and broadcasts on public law issues in both English and Welsh. He was, while at Swansea, Module Director for two innovative undergraduate modules on Legislation and the Law of Multi-Level Governance as well as contributing to Public Law teaching in both English and Welsh. He is the author of a Welsh language work on Public Law – *Sylfeini'r Gyfraith Gyhoeddus* (Foundations of Public Law) commissioned by Bangor University and the Coleg Cymraeg Cenedlaethol (the National Welsh Language College). His teaching and research interests include the legal rights of linguistic and cultural groups, federal and quasi-federal states and non-territorial constitutional structures. At Cardiff, he is a member of the team teaching higher degree Modules on Constitutionalism and Governance and the Law of Devolution in Wales. He was appointed Queen's Counsel (Honoris Causa) in 2014 in recognition of his contribution to increasing public knowledge of Welsh law.

Professor Thomas Glyn Watkin QC (Hon) is a legal academic and former senior civil servant. Before retiring in 2010, he was successively Professor of Law at Cardiff (2001-04) and Bangor (2004-07), and First Legislative Counsel to the Welsh Government (2007-10). A native of Cwmparc in the Rhondda, he was educated at Porth County Grammar School and Pembroke College, Oxford. He was called to the bar by the Middle Temple in 1976 and became a Bencher in 2016. From 1975, he lectured at Cardiff Law School, becoming professor of law in 2001. From 1981 until 1998, he combined his academic work with drafting legislation for the Church in Wales. In 2004, he was appointed professor and head of the new law school at Bangor, before returning to Cardiff and legislative drafting in 2007 as First Legislative Counsel. His principal interest has been legal history, and he has lectured or been a visiting professor at universities in Italy, Spain, Germany, Japan and the United States. His published works include *The Italian Legal Tradition* (1997), *An Historical Introduction to Modern Civil Law* (1999) and *The Legal History of Wales* (2nd ed, 2012). His most recent book, *Legislating for Wales* (with Daniel Greenberg), was published by the University of Wales Press in 2019 as part of its Public Law of Wales series, of which he is General Editor. He remains active in retirement as literary director of the Welsh Legal History Society, for which he has edited nine volumes of essays, and frequently gives evidence on devolution issues to bodies such as committees of the National Assembly for Wales. He is a council member of the Selden Society, a member of the Law Commission's Advisory Committee for Wales, a Fellow of the Learned Society of Wales and a trustee of the Hamlyn Trust. He was appointed an honorary Queen's Counsel in 2019. Married with one daughter, he is also a non-stipendiary priest in the Church in Wales.

Commission Secretariat

John Osmond (Secretary) is Plaid Cymru's Director of Policy and Special Adviser to Adam Price, leader of the party.

Emily Edwards (Research and administration) is Plaid Cymru's Head of Policy.

Endnotes

[1] The chapters of the 'acquis' (presently 35) form the basis of the accession negotiations for each candidate country. They correspond to the different areas of the *acquis* for which reforms are needed in order to meet the accession conditions. The candidate countries are required to adapt their administrative and institutional infrastructures and to bring their national legislation into line with EU legislation in these areas. The chapters range from free movement of goods, workers and capital, to food safety, consumer and health protection, taxation, economic and monetary policy, and the customs union.

[2] Ron Davies, 'Devolution: A Process not an Event', IWA Gregynog Papers, 1998.

[3] This analysis follows that outlined by David Torrance, *"A process not an event": Devolution in Wales, 1998-2020*, House of Commons Library Briefing Paper, 6 April 2020.

[4] Independent Commission on Funding & Finance in Wales, Final Report: 'Fairness and accountability: a new funding settlement for Wales', July 2010, p5.

[5] 'Justice in Wales for the People of Wales', para 2.44, October 2019.

[6] Constitutional and Legislative Affairs Committee, 'Report on the UK Government's Wales Bill', October 2016, p57.

[7] National Assembly for Wales, Expert Panel on Assembly Electoral Reform, 'A Parliament that works for Wales', 12 December 2017.

8   Labour Welsh Government, 'Reforming Our Union: Shared Governance in the UK', September 2019.

9   Theodore Huckle, 'Why Wales Needs its Own Legal Jurisdiction' (07/04/2016) Institute of Welsh Affairs www. iwa.wales/agenda/2016/04/why-wales-needs-its-own-legal-jurisdiction/ accessed 07/07/2020.

10 Scotland Act 1998, ss 28(1) and 29 and 54, sch 5.

11 Northern Ireland Act 1998, s 6 and schs 2 and 3.

12 Government of Wales Act 1998, s 22.

13 *ibid.*, s 1(2).

14 Government of Wales Act 2006, Pts 3 and 4.

15 Wales Act 2014, Pt 4A.

16 Wales Act 2017, s 3(1).

17 *ibid.*, sch 1 s 8.

18 The Commission on Justice in Wales report, *Justice in Wales for the People of Wales* (The Commission on Justice in Wales, October 2019) Executive Summary para 27.

19 Thomas Glyn Watkin with Daniel Greenberg, *Legislating for Wales* (UWP 2018) 242 para A-03.

20 Law Commission, *Form and Accessibility of the Law Applicable in Wales* (Law Com No 366, 2016) paras 12.18-12.19.

21 Welsh Affairs Select Committee, *1st Report – Pre-legislative Scrutiny of the Draft Wales Bill* (HC 2015-2016, 449) para 52.

22 *ibid.*, para 47.

23 The Commission on Justice in Wales (n10) Executive Summary para 2.

24 *ibid.*, para 36.

25 Sunday Closing (Wales) Act 1881, 1.

26 Thomas Watkin in evidence to The Commission on Justice in Wales (n10) WS033 para 4.

27 The Commission on Justice in Wales (n10) Executive Summary 29.

28 Lord Thomas of Cwmgiedd, 'The Role of the Judiciary in a Rapidly Changing Wales' (Legal Wales Conference, 11 October 2013) www.judiciary.uk/wp-content/uploads/2015/10/speech-lcj-legal-wales-speech.pdf accessed 07/07/20.

29 The Commission on Justice in Wales (n10) 12.134.

30 *ibid.*, 12.159.

31 *ibid.*, 12.165.

32 *ibid.*, 12.161.

33 The Commission on Justice in Wales (n10) 2.99.

34 Keith Bush in evidence to The Commission on Justice in Wales (n10) WS052.

35 The Commission on Justice in Wales (n10) Executive Summary 3.

36 *ibid.*, 12.71–12.72

37 *ibid*, Recommendation 78.

38 *ibid*, Executive Summary 1.

39 Rachel Lomax, 'Preparing for the Assembly', IWA, *Agenda*, Winter 1997-98.

40 Private submission.

41 Since then it has not risen above 5,500. In March 2020 it was 5,360.

42 Rhodri Morgan, *Check Against Delivery*, Institute of Welsh Politics Annual Lecture, Aberystwyth, November 2000.

43 Sir Adrian Webb, *Machinery of Government*, Unpublished Memorandum prepared for Mark Drakeford AM as incoming First Minister, October 2018, pp2-3.

44 *ibid.*, p6.

45 *ibid.*, p7.

46 *ibid.*, p8.

47 Graeme Guilford, 'Regional Economic Development in Wales: What does Previous Experience tell us about Future

Approaches?' Paper to the Regional Investment in Wales Steering Group, 2019.

48 Gerald Holtham, 'Wales needs collective Cabinet Government', in *New Nation,* Nova Cambria, Spring 2019.

49 Gerald Holtham, 'Industrial Policy and Infrastructure in Wales', in Wales TUC, *Debating Industrial Policy in Wales,* 2016, p26. Following this criticism, First Minister Carwyn Jones established an office for himself, in effect a Cabinet Office. And, as noted, following the devolution of taxation powers a Welsh Treasury was established within the Finance Department. However, it is not clear that there has been any fundamental improvement in coordination as a result of these changes.

50 Rhodri Morgan, Third Anniversary Lecture, National Centre for Public Policy, Swansea University, December 2020. Note: ASPB refers to 'Assembly Sponsored Public Bodies'.

51 Plaid Cymru, Evidence to the Richard Commission, 2003.

52 Sir Jon Shortridge, Evidence to the Richard Commission, 2003. Note: ASPB refers to 'Assembly Sponsored Public Bodies'.

53 https://academiwales.gov.wales/pages/what-we-believe-yr-hyn-rydyn-nin-ei-gredu

54 https://academi-wales-team-storage.s3-eu-west-1.amazonaws.com/corporate/Annual-Report-2018-2019.pdf

55 John Kay, 'Size isn't all that matters for global economies', *Financial Times,* 26 November 2003.

56 Mark Barry, 'What sort of Wales do we want?', *Nation.Cymru,* 8 March 2020.

57 UK2070 Commission, 'Fairer and Stronger. Rebalancing the UK Economy', May 2019.

58 Guto Ifan, Cian Sion, and Ed Poole, 'Wales' Fiscal Future: A Path to Sustainability?' Wales Governance Centre, Cardiff University, March 2020.

[59] 'Wales' Fiscal Future', *ibid.*, p35.

[60] John Ball, 'The Economics of an Independent Wales', *ClickonWales*, 23 January 2020.

[61] Grahame Guilford, Hywel Ceri Jones and Gaynor Richards, 'Europe Matters to Wales, EU policy and Funding Opportunities, Final Report and Recommendations to the Minister of Finance and Government Business', March 2016.

[62] John Palmer, 'An economic, as well as a monetary union', *socialeurope.eu*, 22 July 2020.

[63] Written Statement by Jeremy Miles, Counsel General and Brexit Minister 20 January, 2020.

[64] Quoted in Welsh Higher Education Board submission to Welsh Government consultation on regional investment funds post Brexit 2020.

[65] 'The European Structural and Investment Funds – contribution to UK research and innovation', published jointly by the British Academy, Learned Society of Wales, Royal Society of Edinburgh, Royal Irish Academy.

[66] This section is based upon Rachel Minto and Kevin Morgan, 'The International Relations of sub-states: Wales in Europe', *The Edinburgh Law Review,* Vol 23, 2019.

[67] Professor Gerald Holtham is the source of this suggestion.

[68] Presentation by Dr Hywel Ceri Jones to the European Parliament's Conference on Funding the EU and EU Funding for Wales, held in Cardiff on 19 April 2013.

[69] Welsh Higher Education Board *op cit.* This last is in stark contrast to the Welsh Government's scatter-gun approach to the use of European funding.

[70] Basque-Wales Innovation Workshops, Bilbao, 26-27 February 2020.

[71] The chapters of the 'acquis' (presently 35) form the basis of the accession negotiations for each candidate country. They

correspond to the different areas of the *acquis* for which reforms are needed in order to meet the accession conditions. The candidate countries are required to adapt their administrative and institutional infrastructures and to bring their national legislation into line with EU legislation in these areas. The chapters range from free movement of goods, workers and capital, to food safety, consumer and health protection taxation, economic and monetary policy, and the customs union.

[72] See House of Lords Library Briefing, 'Constitution, Democracy and Rights Commission', 26 March 2020.

[73] *Scottish Daily Record*, 6 April 2020. It is noteworthy that the commitment was limited to these two sentences. It is noteworthy, too that they were made in the Scottish Press – doubtless as an attempt to strengthen Labour's hand against the SNP. The Labour Party has been silent on the issue since this short announcement.

[74] See the Group's website: www.constitutionreform group. co.uk It includes a number of well-known politicians, and not just members of the House of Lords. Sir Paul Silk, who chaired the Commission on Devolution in Wales, whose final report was published in March 2014, is a prominent member of the Group.

[75] Craig Dalzell and Isobel Lindsay, 'An Unequal Kingdom: The Barriers to Federalism in the UK', Common Weal, April 2018.

[76] The boundaries are those used by the UK Office for National Statistics: North-East, North-West, Yorkshire and the Humber, East Midlands, West Midlands, East of England, Greater London, South-East, South-West.

[77] This point was made very early in the devolution debate by Enoch Powell in a speech at Llwynypia, Rhondda, in May 1974, "Devolution is not the same as the transfer of power; it is the opposite: power devolved is power retained, and that

retention is the very reason which makes devolution acceptable and possible."

[78] Gwynfor Evans, *Diwedd Prydeindod,* 1982, p142.

[79] Adam Price, 'Benelux Britain – Recasting relations in a post-independence era', speech to the Centre on Constitutional Change, Edinburgh University, 26 June 2019.

[80] Glyndwr Cennydd Jones, 'A Federation or League of the Isles' in 'Towards Federalism and Beyond', September 2017; and 'These Isles', Institute of Welsh Affairs 2019.

[81] Adam Price, op.cit.

[82] The Visegrad Group, comprising Poland, Hungary, the Czech Republic, and Slovakia was established in 1991 to advance military, economic, energy and cultural co-operation and to further their integration with the EU.

[83] Adam Price, *op cit.*

[84] Adam Price, 'Wales 2030: Seven Steps to Independence', August 2018.

[85] Edinburgh University Centre on European Relations, 'An Independent Scotland in the EU: issues for accession', March 2020.

[86] See Fabian Zuleeg (Director of the European Policy Centre, Brussels), 'Transition from the UK and to the EU', Scottish Centre on European Relations, 17 March 2020.

[87] www.constitutionreformgroup.co.uk/publications-2/   See also the article by Jim Sillars, 'Is Scotland ready for its federated future to infinity and beyond?', *Scottish Left Review*, March/April 2020.

[88] According to the latest statistics from the Welsh Government's 'Trade Survey for Wales' in 2018, Welsh businesses in Wales sold goods and services to the value of £72.1bn and £29.2bn respectively. The European Union (excluding UK) accounted for 12% of all sales value and the rest of the world accounted

for 8%. 30% of sales went to other parts of the UK, with the balance (50%) distributed within Wales. Businesses in Wales purchased goods and services to the value of £53.4bn and £13.8bn respectively. The European Union (excluding UK) accounted for 13% of all purchase value and the rest of the world accounted for 5%. 51% of purchases were from other parts of the UK.

[89] GoWA 2006 (as amended), schedule 7A, Part 1, para 1(b).

[90] GoWA 2006, schedule 7A, Part 1, para 8.

[91] The Senedd is subject to a General Restriction preventing it from legislating to confer or impose functions upon Ministers of the Crown (being 'a reserved authority') without the consent of 'the appropriate Minister', usually the Secretary of State: GoWA 2006 (as amended), Schedule 7B, para 8(1), (3), (5).

[92] See further, 'Elements of a Welsh Constitution' in the previous chapter, page 162.

[93] Adam Price, 'Wales 2030: Seven Steps to Independence', August 2018.